Jesus, the Best Capernaum Folk-Healer

Jesus, the Best Capernaum Folk-Healer

Mark's Aretalogy of Jesus in the Healing Stories

By
ZORODZAI DUBE

☙PICKWICK *Publications* • Eugene, Oregon

JESUS, THE BEST CAPERNAUM FOLK-HEALER
Mark's Aretalogy of Jesus in the Healing Stories

Copyright © 2020 Zorodzai Dube. All rights reserved. Except for brief quotations in critical publications or reviews, no part of this book may be reproduced in any manner without prior written permission from the publisher. Write: Permissions, Wipf and Stock Publishers, 199 W. 8th Ave., Suite 3, Eugene, OR 97401.

Pickwick Publications
An Imprint of Wipf and Stock Publishers
199 W. 8th Ave., Suite 3
Eugene, OR 97401

www.wipfandstock.com

PAPERBACK ISBN: 978-1-7252-8080-9
HARDCOVER ISBN: 978-1-7252-8079-3
EBOOK ISBN: 978-1-7252-8081-6

Cataloguing-in-Publication data:

Names: Dube, Zorodzai

Title: Jesus, the best Capernaum folk-healer : Mark's aretology of Jesus in the healing stories / by Zorodzai Dube.

Description: Eugene, OR: Pickwick Publications, 2020 | Includes bibliographical references.

Identifiers: ISBN 978-1-7252-8080-9 (paperback) | ISBN 978-1-7252-8079-3 (hardcover) | ISBN 978-1-7252-8081-6 (ebook)

Subjects: LCSH: Bible. Mark—Criticism, interpretation, etc. | Healing—Biblical teaching. | Public worship. | Jesus Christ.

Classification: BS2555.6.H4 D83 2020 (print) | BS2555.6.H4 (ebook)

Manufactured in the U.S.A.   NOVEMBER 6, 2020

To Professor Halvor Moxnes—my mentor—to you, I hope that the hypothesis and arguments contained herein are "plausible."

In gods, we shall first venerate the majesty of their nature in general terms, and then the power of each individually and any inventions which have given useful service to mankind. Thus the power of Jupiter will be shown to consist in ruling all things, that of Mars in war, that of Neptune in his control of the sea. Similarly with inventions: Minerva has the arts, Mercury letters, Apollo medicine, Ceres corn, and Bacchus wine. Next come any actions that antiquity attributes to them; while honour is also added to gods by parentage (e.g., if one is the child of Jupiter), by age (as with those born of Chaos), and finally by their offspring (as Apollo and Diana lend honour to Latona). It is grounds for praise in some of them that they were born immortal, and in others that they achieved immortality by their virtues.

—Quintilian, *Inst.* 3.7.7; trans. Russell et al., 2016:23

Contents

Acknowledgments | ix
Abbreviations | x

Chapter 1
Aim, Objectives, and Literature Review | 1

Chapter 2
The Ndau's Dondo People as Indirect Analogue of Praise-Giving | 17

Chapter 3
Heroes and Gods as Direct Praise-Giving Analogue in Greco-Roman Society | 43

Chapter 4
Mark's Gospel and Jesus' Household as Site of Healing | 77

Chapter 5
Mark and Aretalogy concerning the Best Folk Healer—Jesus | 101

Chapter 6
Healing Praise-Giving within African Pentecostal Churches | 146

Chapter 7
Concluding Remarks | 163

Bibliography | 167

Acknowledgments

I THANK MY MOTHER, the daughter to the great Dondo chief and healer Musikavanhu, for providing songs and insights into rituals concerning installation of a chief. She also explained various rituals performed when approaching a traditional healer. I also thank my sisters, Constance Chitakatira, Margret Dube, Thelma Dube, Ndakadini Dube, Charity Dube, and Talent Dube, and my brother Kumbirai Dube from Chipinge for providing complementary information regarding rituals associated with the installation of a chief and rituals observed when approaching a traditional healer. Brighton Dube, thank you for assisting in proofreading and with an eagle's eye, you managed to pick up typos within the manuscript. In addition, I thank Professors Halvor Moxnes and Anna Rebecca Solevåg from the University of Oslo in Norway for critically reading and inserting valuable comments to the manuscript. This project began with the encouragement from my friend Professor Elia Shabani Mligo from Teofilo Kisanji University in Mbeya, Tanzania; I thank him for pushing and encouraging me to start this book project.

Abbreviations

BCE   Before the Common Era
CE   Common Era
ECG   Enlightened Christian Gathering
HIV   Human Immunodeficiency Virus

Chapter 1

Aim, Objectives, and Literature Review

INTRODUCTION

THIS BOOK TAKES THE established fields of orality, performance, and first-century Christian health-care studies further by using analogues of praise performances to Apollo, Asclepius, and those from the Dondo people of southeastern Zimbabwe to propose that Jesus' healing stories in Mark's gospel are praise-giving narratives to Jesus as the best folk healer within the region of Capernaum. The book proposes that the memory of Jesus as the folk healer from Capernaum survived and possibly functioned in similar contexts of praise-giving within early Christian households. Importantly, the existence of Asclepius's shrines across Palestine and in places very close or similar to where Jesus lived, such as Hammath, Emmaus, the Sea of Galilee, Neapolis, Ascalon, Magdala, and Bethsaida,[1] provides a plausible comparable link between the memory concerning Jesus' healing and that of other healers in the region. Given this, I suggest that the memory regarding Jesus as a healer competed with healing memories concerning other healers in the region. Telling and repeating Jesus' healing memory within the early Christian household close to those of Asclepius at Tiberius, Gadara (Hammet Gader) plausibly functioned (i) to spread the fame of Jesus as a healer vis-à-vis other healers in the region and (ii) as internal and external identity formation seeking to instil collective belief that the healer from Nazareth was the best healer.

1. The village of Bethsaida located at the eastern coast of the Lake of Galilee should not be confused with Bethesda, a village close to Jerusalem.

Jesus, the Best Capernaum Folk-Healer

Theoretically, the study builds upon form criticism research by Martin Dibelius and Rudolf Bultmann, who suggest that the various narratives that exist in the New Testament circulated independent from each other and then were later collected into larger narrative units.[2] To build on this hypothesis, this study utilizes two models—first, praise-giving performances given to traditional chiefs and traditional healers among the Dondo people of southeastern Zimbabwe (as indirect analogue). Second, the praise-giving performances toward Greco-Roman healers such as Apollo and Asclepius are used as direct analogues. Both the direct and indirect analogues are combined and used as interpretive paradigms to infer the possible context around which Mark's healing stories were performed within early Jesus households in Capernaum. Throughout the text, I use the term *paean* interchangeably with praise-giving choral / victory ode. Etymologically in Greek mythology, the term *paean* was synonymous with the Olympian healing god Apollo and his son Asclepius. I also use the term *aretalogy* interchangeably with the phrase "praise-giving." By taking the praise-giving performances associated with various gods and heroes within the Greco-Roman world and combining this with analogue of praise-giving among the Dondo people of southeastern Zimbabwe, this study rereads Mark's healing narratives as performative praise-giving stories.

HYPOTHESIS

Unlike our contemporary context, where healing stories are read and listened to by a sitting audience in a church, healing activities at shrines of Apollo, Dionysus, Demeter, Apollo, and Asclepius were accompanied by choral songs and dance celebrations. They were publicly danced out and orally delivered. In most shrines, visitors arrived at the shrine singing and carrying various gifts to their gods. As seen later in chapter 3, the culture of celebrating the heroes at stadiums and amphitheaters was not exclusive to honoring the gods that made the victory possible. In most cases, the victory praise song to the winner at the Panhellenic games would simultaneously praise the winner and the god(s) at the same time. *Paeans* accompanied by dance and chorus music characterized the mood at most shrines.

Unlike many of today's worship services, Greco-Roman gods were not worshipped in silence. Instead, their fame and identity were celebrated

---

2. Bultmann, "New Approach to the Synoptic Problem," 337; Dibelius, *Fresh Approach to the New Testament.*

Aim, Objectives, and Literature Review

by the noise and praise-giving that chronicled their benevolent deeds to their followers. Vernon McCasland in *The Asklepios Cult in Palestine* and Megan Nutzman in "In This Holy Place" established that the shrines of Asclepius together with his sons Machaon and Podalirius were dotted throughout Palestine.[3] Evidence of coins with the image of Hygieia—the healing daughter of Asclepius—were excavated in Tiberius, indicating the existence of a thriving worship center in that region. In addition, places such as Hammath, Emmaus, the Sea of Galilee, Neapolis, Ascalon, Bethsaida, Magdala, and Bethsaida all have vibrant Asclepius shrines.[4] Acknowledging the existence of Asclepius shrines in places such as Gadara, Bethsaida, and Tiberius, locations very close to Capernaum, it is plausible to assume that forms of worship associated with Asclepius were known to Jesus' household in Capernaum. In Mark's gospel, as we shall see in chapter 5, Jesus had been to Tiberius, where synagogues exist alongside a thermal miracle spring. With full knowledge of the healing powers associated with the pool at Tiberius and Gadara, Jesus may have drawn large pool for sick people who waited healing from such sites. This may indicate that Jesus and his followers may have full knowledge of other healing gods. Furthermore, Asclepius was far more famous as a healer compared to Jesus, making the temptation to consult him very irresistible. In antiquity, depending on one's needs, religion was an open market and people were free to visit whichever god they prefer or trust. Attending a shrine of a god would not preclude going to the shrine of the other gods. However, Jews and their schismatic cousins, the Christians, were monolatry religions who believed in one supreme being, Yahweh, as healer. However, not wanting to present the Jews as religiously strict and closed from other religious, Hector Avalos reveals figurines of other non-Yahweh gods which could be attributed to the demise of the prophetic office in the second temple.[5] Megan Nutzman makes similar claim that all ethnicities including the Jews visited the magical thermal pool.[6] Therefore, this book revisits Martin Dibelius and Rudolf Bultmann's form critical approach by taking their approach further to suggest that healing *paeans* and dances associated with many Greco-Roman

---

3. McCasland, "Asklepios Cult in Palestine," 221–27; Nutzman, "In This Holy Place," 281.

4. McCasland, "Asklepios Cult in Palestine," 227.

5. Avalos, *Health Care and the Rise of Christianity*, 39.

6. Nutzman, "In This Holy Place," 281.

gods could be plausible analogues in reconstructing the manner the healing stories were performed.

The hypothesis of this book is supported by two main assumptions:

- First, as proposed by Hector Avalos, early Christianity spread primarily as a healing religion.[7] This proposal is not far to see when one reads the gospel stories and Acts whose, among many, main narrative prosthesis is the miracles that attracted people to the new religion.[8] Religion and healing were inseparable. In fact, religious shrines were primarily health-care centers using various instruments such as divination, herbs, and ritual baths for healing.

- Second, as we have already alluded, the proximity of healing shrines of Asclepius in areas such as Hammath, Emmaus, the Sea of Galilee, Neapolis, Ascalon, Bethsaida, Magdala, and Bethsaida are a plausible link between Mark's memory of Jesus as the healer and the existence of competing healers.

MOTIVATION

This study is motivated by interest in social scientific reading of the New Testament writings that takes seriously social context from which the New Testament literatures came. Bruce Malina and John Pilch remark that reading the New Testament writings are similar to taking a journey to a foreign land from which the traveler faces the challenge of an emic interpretation concerning what one reads or sees.[9] In this regard, the healing stories are some of the activities performed by Jesus that are difficult to imagine their emic perspective. Martin Dibelius and Rudolf Bultmann regard the stories as having developed from early Christian missionaries and controversies with the religious leaders, respectively. I take this perspective further by seeking to understand how they were performed. By putting the stories at the beginning of his narrative about Jesus, Mark gives a clue concerning the fact that the stories were known and crucial items to the early church. Some of the healing stories celebrated by Mark are the healing of the demoniac in the synagogue, the healing of Peter's mother-in-law, the healing of many

---

7. Avalos, *Health Care and the Rise of Christianity*, 82.
8. Theissen, *Gospels in Context*.
9. Malina, *Social Gospel of Jesus*; Pilch, *Healing in the New Testament*.

people who gathered at Peter's mother-in-law's house during the evening, the healings across Nazareth and Capernaum, and the healing of a man with leprosy. Throughout Mark's gospel, several healing stories were also recorded provoking the reader concerning how such stories were told and remembered. There is need for an emic interpretation based on observations of similar stories found in the region. To take the form of a sitting and listening audience as we do each Sunday may result in missing the possible performance accompanying the delivery and memory of the stories. If we assume a community behind the stories and that Jesus was the focus of the healing memory, then how were these stories delivered and performed and what identity implication associated with Jesus or the community is assumed by such memory?

The second motivation comes from the need for an interdisciplinary reading of the stories from the perspective of praise-giving analogues. Among the Dondo people of southeastern Zimbabwe, healing and good deeds are celebrated through songs of various forms of totemic poetry. Equally, similar practices exist among Greco-Roman societies in the form of cultic festival, poetry, and *paeans* to gods and heroes. The immediate rebuttal toward such motivation would be how contemporary analogues from the Dondo people assist in reading such ancient stories. In response, Malina and Pilch developed ideas from archaeology to argue that indirect analogues may provide comparative interpretive tools to understand an ancient text.[10] In most Southern African societies, traditional healers provide crucial folk healing services and in return, communities sing songs in praise of their healing powers. More detail regarding this is given in chapter 2. While approaching a shrine of a healer, songs and gestures of praise and reverence are performed. From a rather person perspective, I grew up observing my uncle, a great traditional healer from the Dondo tribe. Besides being a healer, my uncle's clan holds the chieftaincy of the area. I grew up observing people coming to my uncle's homestead for healing or seeking charms for good fortunes. From a distance of 100 meters toward his homestead, it was customary for the visitors to start reciting his totemic poem or sing praise-song in his honor.

Equally, African Pentecostal churches who borrow heavily from African independent churches and African traditional healers perform healing as main part of their church services. In chapter 6, we shall look at praise-giving and healing performances with specific reference to the practices of

---

10. Malina, *Social Gospel of Jesus*; Pilch, *Healing in the New Testament*.

the Enlightened Christian Gathering (ECG) Church led by Prophet Sheppard Bushiri. In fact a three-stage pattern is observable, which is: (i) a healer with stronger healing power or source (ii) heals several complicated ailments and (iii) is followed by many people. The reverse to this statement is true, which is: (i) the level of praise-giving (*paean*) is (ii) dependent of the nature of ailments which the healer can heal and (iii) based on the nature of power used by the healer. Due to lack of cheaper and available hospitals, African Pentecostal church services are occasions to demonstrate healing power.[11] Every Sunday, African preachers compete over who performs the most outrageous miracles. For example, to outshine fellow preachers, Prophet Alpha Lukau of Alleluia Ministries International was alleged to have resurrected a dead man back to life.[12] In the video that can be found online, Lukau seems to be emphasizing that the dead person brought to him was retrieved from the mortuary for burial. After receiving backlash from mortuaries that accused the prophet for falsely implicating them in his miracles, Lukau later recanted, saying he was merely repeating what the relatives of the dead man had told him. Other preachers have even gone to extent of feeding people grass, dog meat and rats, cajoling their adherents that such weird practices would results in transmission of miracles into their lives. It seems that the more weird or unbelievable the miracle, the more people flock to the preacher.

CONTRIBUTION, AIM, AND OBJECTIVES

This book builds upon the existing literature regarding orality and performance by scholars such as David Rhoads[13] by bringing in the analogical themes from praise performances among the Dondo people of southeastern Zimbabwe and Greco-Roman victory odes and cultic performances. It assumes that the contexts of oral performances at shrines of various gods across the empire and within Palestine are plausible settings for reading the healing stories.

Furthermore, while reading the healing stories as praise-giving performances, this book further builds on existing discussions regarding Jewish and Christian health-care systems by complementing and illustrating insights from medical anthropologists such as Hector Avalos. The healing

---

11. Cebelihle, "It's a Miracle."
12. Seleka, "Hoax Resurrection."
13. Rhoads, "Performance Criticism," 121.

stories do not only reflect the Judeo-Christian personalistic worldview but, more importantly, they demonstrate that more and more people were attracted to Christianity as the alternative health-care system because of its renewal of monolatry in Yahweh as the only God; its simple request for prayer and faith among others as conditions for healing. Thus, in reading Jesus as the best Capernaum folk healer, we are called upon to reflect on how Christianity renewed Jewish health-care system by becoming the host and hospital for a majority of people who had been denied restoration by the Jewish health-care system. Thus, the celebrations gleaned from reading each story should be understood as praise over finding an alternative healer in Jesus who heals through mere rituals of touch, command, or request for faith and prayer. By receiving instant healing that does not require laborious rituals or a period of waiting, their celebration attracted more people who were in similar predicaments. To these, indeed, Jesus is the best Capernaum folk healer.

LITERATURE REVIEW CONCERNING HEALING STORIES

Social Scientific Perspectives

Social scientific criticism is interested in social life, norm, and cultural patterns reflected through the biblical narratives.[14] It focuses on the social world, culture, political, economic and social context of Palestine. Healing stories fall within the category of social life and several interpretations have been given regarding the meaning of the healing stories in Mark's gospel. Scholars such as Janna Dewey and Halvor Moxnes see healing as a social aspect within the broader context of empire and temple rituals.[15] For them the Jesus movement grew within a context of social upheaval caused by the presence of empire and the temple and internal domestic challenges caused by the rules implemented by the patriarchy. While the empire took land from the peasants and charged extra temple tax, the household had cultural rules that were difficult for the sick, the widows, and those with contagious conditions. As we shall develop in chapter 4, the Jesus movement that developed in Capernaum offered alternative space for hospitality

---

14. Elliott, "What Is Social-Scientific Criticism?"
15. Dewey, "Survival of Mark's Gospel," 495; Moxnes, *Putting Jesus in His Place*.

Jesus, the Best Capernaum Folk-Healer

and commensality. According to Joanna Dewey and David Rhoads, in opposition to the temple and empire, Jesus formed the household as space for teaching, exorcism, and healing.[16] Mark uses the healing stories to signify the arrival of an alternative kingdom whose mission is restoration of the sick, outcast, and oppressed. From this perspective, Mark's healing stories are restorative in nature.[17] Importantly, from this perspective, the conceptualization of healing is as social restoration and not merely biomedical. Instead healing is a social restorative activity that includes hospitality and commensality.[18]

Besides the social restorative aspect of healing, scholars such as Peter Craffert appeal to comparative models of healers found in the Mediterranean region.[19] One such model is that during Jesus' times, several men of God (*theo aner*) known for possessing divine healing power existed. For example, Apollonia of Tyna, Hanina Ben Dorsa, and Honi the "Circle Drawer" had power to heal and perform extraordinary acts. For example, Honi the Circle Drawer had ability to command rain during draught. Taking this direction, Pieter Craffert uses an indirect analogy of a shaman to argue that Jesus perform similar roles as that of a shaman. A shaman is a healer that uses supernatural powers derived from his spiritual worldview. To the community, he/she can command rain or predict the future regarding immediate events.[20]

Within the African context, the shaman type is similar to a sangoma, especially the diviner kind. Sangomas exist in three types—the diviner *sangoma* who has spiritual powers to tap into the mysteries of divine power. The second type is the *herbalist type*—this one has vast inherited knowledge regarding herbs. The last type is the *lot-caster*—this type casts lot and through divine power is able to tell the client the kind of problem he/she is facing. Notably, most sangomas can operate in all three modes—the diviner, lot caster and herbalist. The main variable or starting point in this perspective is acknowledging the supernatural power within the individual. Using the shaman model, it is possible to argue that, through his healing activities,

---

16. Rhoads et al., *Mark as Story*; Dewey, "Survival of Mark's Gospel"; Dewey, "Oral Methods of Structuring Narrative in Mark," 32–44.

17. Van Eck, "Galilea En Jerusalem as Narratologiese," 139–63; Moxnes, *Putting Jesus in His Place*.

18. Crossan, *Historical Jesus*.

19. Craffert, *Life of a Galilean Shaman*.

20. Craffert, *Life of a Galilean Shaman*.

Jesus presented himself as one endowed with divine power which he uses over all kinds of sickness and nature.

Theological Perspective

Throughout history, the theological view is the dominant perspective. Unlike the shaman model, the theological perspective starts its reasoning regarding the healing stories by acknowledging the divinity of Jesus and his identity as equal or coming from God. In most areas where it is used, the theological perspective, anachronistically, drags christological themes to Jesus, arguing that his ability to heal was evidence of manifestation of his divinity as God. The argument runs as follows: given that Jesus was God incarnate, therefore miracles demonstrated his identity as God. Similarly, the exorcisms are demonstration of superior divine power over demonic powers that caused illness. Taking this perspective, the entire ministry of Jesus is reduced to two groups of people—those similar to the religious leaders who opposed or doubted Jesus' identity as God's envoy and then those with faith that perceived in Jesus his divine origin. Howard Clark Kee and Hendrik Van der Loos are representatives of this position.[21] Emphasis on Jesus, which almost removes him from his larger context, is the major criticism given to this position. By failing to give due diligence toward other healers, this perspective fails to realize that Jesus was not the only healer. Consequently, the perspective does not locate the healing miracles of Jesus within larger context of healing practitioners within the region.

Psychological Perspective

However not the last in terms of importance and relevance, the psychological perspective is one major lens used to explain the healing stories. The discursive starting point of this perspective is acknowledging the universality of patterns of sickness and yet a realization that modernity and rationality changed our mindset regarding sickness. Using modern understanding, the perspective seeks to make sense of healing stories from the perspective of modern knowledge regarding health and healing. We can use modern knowledge of sickness to explain various conditions narrated in the Bible. Gerd Theissen, the representative of this category, says that Jesus' healing

---

21. Kee, *Community of the New Age*; Van der Loos, *Miracles of Jesus*.

miracles had placebo effect embedded into the religious cultural worldview of the people.[22] By use of the cultural symbolic interpretation to illness, Jesus gave cultural symbolic meaning to sickness by interpreting illness from the perspective of the spirit world. Upon getting sick, the person asks himself/herself "why"—thus looking for the deeper spiritual meaning of the sickness. John Pilch calls such mindset—personalistic worldview which differs from biomedical or naturalistic understanding of the world based on search for cure.[23] From this perspective, New Testament sickness conditions such as demon possession are redescribed using comparative and modern descriptions such as epilepsy or schizophrenia.

Other scholars within this category combine psychological perspective and the political and economic condition of the people during the New Testament times. In doing this, they assume that people who experience extreme socioeconomic pressure exhibit certain mental conditions and sometimes even mental illness. For example, Richard Horsley and Ched Meyers are representative voices of this perspective and both argue that first-century Palestine experienced political pressure from the empire, which resulted in them being landless.[24] However, given that scholars such as Jean Freyne note that the first half of the first century characterized by economic boom during Emperor Tiberius's reign was generally peaceful and then followed by a more volatile period after the reign of Emperor Nero, the description of violence and instability needs to be presented with caution.[25] In agreement with Josephus's representation of Galilee, subsistence rural peasants inhabited the region of Galilee and by taking land from them; it meant the collapse of their ability to subsist and the end of their social network ties.[26] In addition, the consequence of being landless resulted in a majority of peasants resorting to being tenants at the farms of landowners, which resulted in paying high taxes in form of grain. Failure to pay tax would, in some cases, result in the entire family being taken as slaves. Interpreting Jesus' parable of the Tenant in the Vineyard, John Kloppenborg remarks that landlords benefited from tax extraction from the tenants. The discovery of grain silo and weights in Tiberius further proves the prevalence of the

---

22. Van Horn, "By Whose Authority?"
23. Pilch, *Healing in the New Testament*, 58.
24. Horsley, *Hearing the Whole Story*; Myers, *Binding the Strong Man*.
25. Freyne, "Galileans in the Light of Josephus' Vita," 397; Freyne, "Herodian Economics in Galilee," 23–46.
26. Oakman, *Jesus and the Peasants*, 74.

system of tenancy and landownership.²⁷ Psychologically, such economic and social pressure would result in mental illness. From the perspective of trauma theory the exorcism and healing stories could be understood as trauma intervention stories that seeks to give alternative meaning-making narrative within a context of political and economic pressure.²⁸

While this perspective raises human response to social challenges, it has its own weaknesses. One of the challenges being that psychological perspective is an etic and redactive approach that seeks to reinterpret the way ancient people view reality using science. The ancient Mediterranean worldview concerning sickness is emic and should be understood from the perspective of an insider. Hence, using modern lenses to reinterpret events concerning the past may result in missing the emic cultural meaning-making frameworks.

THEORATICAL PERSPECTIVES

In their present form, the healing stories in Mark's gospel are written stories removed from their original context of oral performance, gossip, laughter, dancing and possible jubilation that comes from witnessing the healing. In trying to reconstitute their emic standpoint, I shall use a number of social scientific perspective to reanimate the healing stories as oral and performative narratives. In doing this, I concur with John Pilch's remark that "increasing number of scholars draw upon a number of social methods to supplement and enhance the other exegetical tools."²⁹ The following theoretical perspective of form and reduction criticism, performance, festival and orality are helpful tools in investigating the various angles from which we can understand the performance and form of the healing stories.

Form and Redaction Criticism

We shall use redaction and form criticism to explore the process of formation of the current healing stories. In using form criticism, we meet two frequent terms—*Sitz im Leben* and *pericope*. *Sitz im Leben*, which refers to specific context from which a particular story emerges. *Pericope* refers to

---

27. Kloppenborg, *Tenants in the Vineyard*, 331.
28. Dube, "Storytelling in time of violence," 192.
29. Pilch, *Healing in the New Testament*, 58.

the existence of separate independent narratives that were later redacted into the final story. It aims to recover the original form of context from which the biblical text originated. In saying this, it assumes that the current various stories about healing were taken from a particular setting relating to healing.[30] Concerning the Gospel of Mark, form criticism makes us appreciate that the healing stories originated separately from the rest of Mark's narrative. Form criticism assumes that what we have in the Bible is a complete and redacted version of various narratives that were taken from different contexts. For example, a form or narrative that came from a cultic or worship context was put together with a form or narrative concerning conflict or controversy. Such an example is found in the story regarding the healing of a man with withered hand on a Sabbath (Mark 3:1–6).

In Mark's gospel, five pericopes that build the Gospel of Mark are noticeable: the parable stories, the healing stories, the controversy stories, the sea crossing stories, and the crucifixion stories. Martin Dibelius suggests that the healing stories originated from a context of early church preaching or missionary work and, in such contexts, the stories functioned as paradigms or examples that illustrated Jesus' power. For example, the stories regarding casting of demons or healing of the sick were meant to evoke faith in Jesus.[31] To support this, in sending his disciples on the great commission (Mark 16:15–16), Jesus says, "Go into all the world and proclaim the gospel to the whole creation. Whoever believes and is baptized will be saved, but whoever does not believe will be condemned. And these signs will accompany those who believe: in my name they will cast out demons; they will speak in new tongues; they will pick up serpents with their hands; and if they drink any deadly poison, it will not hurt them; they will lay their hands on the sick, and they will recover."

From Jesus' instruction, the performance of miracles such as casting out of demons, picking up serpents, and drinking poison were public demonstrations of power with intention to convert people to the new religion. Rudolf Bultmann came up with slightly different context for the performance of the healing stories. For him, the healing stories arose from settings of controversy between Jesus and Jewish authorities with intent to present Jesus as a better rabbi or teacher. Within such context, the healing stories functioned to counter particular rabbinic teaching regarding the

---

30. Bultmann, "New Approach to the Synoptic Problem," 337.

31. McGinley, "Form-Criticism of the Synoptic Healing Narratives," 451; Dibelius and Woolf, *From Tradition to Gospel*; Dibelius, *Fresh Approach to the New Testament*.

Sabbath, thus revealing Jesus as better teacher.[32] For example, the healing of the man with leprosy evoked debate concerning rabbinic concept of purity (Mark 1:40ff.). In addition, the healing of the paralytic man evoked debate regarding observance of the Sabbath day (Mark 2:1–12). Similarly the debate concerning the Sabbath is the larger narrative frame around which the calling and eating with the sinner Levi (Mark 2:13–17), the debate about fasting (Mark 2:18–22), the plucking of grain on the Sabbath (Mark 2:23–28), and the healing of a man with withered hand on a Sabbath (Mark 3:1–6) are discussed. Using Bultmann's form criticism, we deduce that Mark debated the law concerning Sabbath observance to teach about the torah's teaching regarding love and mercy. In the debate, leaving the legal issues of the torah, Jesus focuses on love and mercy as the spiritual meaning of the torah. This book takes Dibelius and Bultmann's form criticism further by proposing praise-giving in the context of healing and hero worship as plausible comparative context or form to imagine the performance of Mark's healing stories.

Orality

To complement, form and redaction criticism, we should acknowledge that the healing stories circulated as oral stories. Orality studies developed from anthropology with a view to focus our attention to how subsistence communities rely on oral or aural as instrument to share ideas. Perspectives within orality studies range from focus on literary techniques to memory preservation. Anthropologists Milman Perry and Albert Bates Lord using South Slavic epics remarks that Greek epics were orally told and performed publicly.[33] Similarly, John Miles Foley studies Greek novels such as *Iliad* and *Odyssey* and came to a conclusion that folk stories were orally and publicly performed.[34] Following the lead of John Miles Foley, Swedish scholar Birger Gerhardsson investigates how the New Testament writings reveal oral techniques.[35]

The influence of interdisciplinary studies with anthropology and other social sciences shifted earlier focus on oral techniques to orality as

---

32. McGinley, "Form-Criticism of the Synoptic Healing Narratives," 451; Bultmann, "New Approach to the Synoptic Problem," 337.
33. Parry and Parry, *Making of Homeric Verse*, xix.
34. Foley, *Singer of Tales*, 2.
35. Gerhardsson, *Memory and Manuscript*, 34.

memory and identity formation.³⁶ Orality studies immensely influenced our approach of the New Testament writings by making us aware that, when reading the New Testament stories, we are dealing with an aural culture and that, the stories were meant to be told orally to listening audiences. Thus when reading the New Testament healing stories, we need to radically shift from our written text-oriented worldview to storytelling. In addition, given that the New Testament narratives were read publicly and aloud, a shift is needed in viewing these stories as publicly performed and not silently read. Scholars such as Werner Kelber, Thomas Boomershine, and Joana Dewey wrote extensively on this subject.³⁷

Performance Criticism

Orality approach goes together with performance approach. With reference to Paul's letters, David Rhoads and Peter Botha opine that the New Testament writings were publicly performed to an active audience.³⁸ After being written down on a scroll or flat stone and to reproduce the author's own presence, the messenger was coached on how to publicly perform the contents of the letter.³⁹

For Rhoads, the New Testament writings are performed stories—the orator performing to the listening audience who responded to the performance through various expressions.⁴⁰ Rhoads remarks, "Ancient performers composed and recomposed their material in the context of numerous performances before diverse audiences and in the context of differing social circumstances."⁴¹ During the process of performance, "the performers had the responsibility to put their own take on the story, fit it to the immediate audience and situation, and even adjust it to the responses of the audience in the very course of performing."⁴² To aid performance and memory, "the compositions were episodic, redundant (with variation), additive, aggregative, genre-driven, with parallels and contrasts, chiastic patterns, plot

---

36. Draper, *Orality, Literacy, and Colonialism*; Thatcher, *Jesus, the Voice, and the Text*.
37. Kelber, *Mark's Story of Jesus*, 139; Dewey, "Oral Methods of Structuring Narrative," 23; Dewey, "Survival of Mark's Gospel," 495; Gerhardsson, *Memory and Manuscript*.
38. Botha, *Orality and Literacy*.
39. Botha, *Orality and Literacy*, 17.
40. Rhoads et al., *Mark as Story*, 121.
41. Rhoads et al., *Mark as Story*, 121.
42. Rhoads et al., *Mark as Story*, 123.

Aim, Objectives, and Literature Review

markers, mnemonic hook words, and featuring memorable stories, proverbial sayings, and vivid analogies."[43] Having grown up in the rural areas where written literature is not a common way of receiving and sending news, I grew up observing orality and performances. During the evenings, I grew up listening to my mother and grandmother telling stories around the fire. Stories were deductive, teaching us moral lessons through real stories and folk stories. In addition, some stories were meant to entertain and make us laugh as we waited for bedtime. In telling stories, songs and gestures were used to make us remember and enjoy the story. This perspective assists in viewing and imagining how the healing stories circulated as oral stories throughout the village of Capernaum.

Festival Approach

In addition to orality and performance, when words of a community leader are continuously repeated, they become part of community commemorative material. Festivals are periodic community rituals whose function is enacting memory and reinforcing crucial community events or traditions. Anthropologist Jan Assmann discusses festivals from the perspective of memory and identity formation, arguing that communities cultivate their identity through calendrical festivals that include retelling the past to form present identities. Through their repetition which sediment important cultural memory, festivals reveal collective desires, taboos, and aspirations of a community.[44]

In using festival approach, it is possible to explore the healing stories as performative commemorative events celebrating the establishment and identity of the Markan community in Capernaum. Plausibly, during encounters with other healers in the region, they began telling their own stories about their community and its founder. Since most of Jesus' healing performances were done within households, it is plausible that such settings were used to celebrate the community's folk healer. In addition, when facing sickness, the name of Jesus was evoked as ritual of power. For example signifying its ritual power, we see Peter and Paul exorcizing demons in the name of Jesus.[45] Consequently, festival approach assists in investigating the

---

43. Rhoads et al., *Mark as Story*, 124.
44. Assmann and Czaplicka, "Collective Memory and Cultural Identity," 125.
45. Koenig, *Rediscovering New Testament Prayer*.

sedimentation of memory of Jesus as healer and its function in identity formation of early Christianity as healing movement.

CHAPTER DIVISIONS

The book is divided into six chapters. Chapter 1, is introductory material exploring literature review and theoretical perspective, while chapter 2, using forms of praise-giving among the Dondo people of southeastern Zimbabwe, illustrates various forms of praise-giving at the domestic, cultic, and political spaces. In chapter 3, praise-giving in the form of Panhellenic victory choral odes to hero-gods such as Demeter, Apollo, Dionysus, and Asclepius are explained. Chapter 4 looks into the formation and growth of the Jesus movement in the village of Capernaum. The village's geography, social classes, and social issues are discussed in detail. In addition, attention is given to hot thermal baths at various centers such as Gadara and Tiberius and the various deities that were evoked during the ritual baths. From this context, the Jesus movement developed around its identity of Jesus as its healer. Seemingly, by healing many people with various forms of sickness, the Jesus movement grew to compete for attention with other gods in the region. Chapter 5 is the main chapter of the book which, drawing on *paeans* from other healers, demonstrates how Jesus was celebrated as a best folk healer. Each healing story, the cultural stigma or assumptions behind each story and how Jesus' healing was celebrated through the memory of such healing is demonstrated. Chapter 6 contextualizes the discussion by intersecting healing performances and praise-giving in one of the main African Pentecostal churches in South Africa. Field reports of healing performances conducted in Enlightened Christian Gathering Church led by Prophet Shepherd Bushiri are used to demonstrate the argument.

Chapter 2

The Ndau's Dondo People as Indirect Analogue of Praise-Giving

INTRODUCTION

THIS CHAPTER EXPLAINS THE analogical (comparative) method as interpretive approach to read the healing stories in Mark's gospel. As the introduction indicates, using comparative praise-giving performances attributed to other healers, the task of this book is imagining the healing stories in Mark's gospel as praise-giving performances. This chapter explains the analogical method and then, using the Dondo people of southeastern Zimbabwe (a clan within the Ndau people), it highlights the various contexts and forms of praise-giving. Important to note from this chapter is that praise-giving is central to the Dondo people's cosmology as a form of respect and celebrating power and protection. Concerning varied contexts, praise-giving is given in the domestic space as a form of moral encouragement and as a gesture of honoring the chiefs or traditional healers.

WHAT IS ANALOGICAL OR COMPARATIVE METHOD?

Before proceeding, we need to understand the analogical method. The analogical or comparative method is commonly used in academic fields such as archaeology and anthropology where a model/fit is required to approximate data where there is limited information. To do so, it uses two strands, namely: *direct* and *indirect* analogies.[1] Discursively, given the distance from the cultural practices alluded to in the Bible, it assumes that we face the challenge of describing the culture referred to by the biblical narratives. For example, in many contexts, the Bible talks about issues such as honor and shame, agricultural activities, household matters, and politico-economic issues. To assume that our modern technological cultural worldview can conceptualize such a worldview is anachronism. Therefore, the question that might arise is, how do we explain the world behind the biblical texts? As solution, the method relies on comparative models/fits that approximate the situation being investigated.

Comparative models or fits function as heuristic interpretive paradigms. However, two challenges emerge. First, how do we decide concerning the best suitability of model/fit? Second, since a model is a comparative fit, how far should the comparison be taken as comparative tool? Should a particular practice within a chosen model be extracted from a particular culture and used or should we use the entire model? If, for example, the entire cultural practice is selected, are we not conflating cultural practices from a different culture over the other?

What are direct analogues? Inspired by Charles Darwin's evolutionary theory,[2] direct models are derived from cultures that geographically and historical evolve from the same culture(s) as that being studied.[3] For example, in biblical studies, direct analogues are taken from contemporary cultures existing in the Mediterranean region. In using direct models, present cultures who are descendants of past cultures, inherited cultural practices that can be plausibly used to explain the past.[4] Because of perceived continuity with ancient culture, most social scientists prefer direct analogues to indirect analogies. While cultures in the Middle East have changed, scholars such as Bruce Malina studied practices such as honor and shame, subsistence/peasant, and kinship models from the Middle East and regards such as heuristic tools to explaining similar practices reflected in the Bible.[5] A direct analogical perspective takes the models of honor and

---

1. Gould and Watson, "Dialogue on the Meaning and Use of Analogy," 359.

2. Charles Darwin suggests that species, through evolution, develop from simple to complex forms and that their simple forms contain the pure genetic form uncorrupted by time and cultural or genetic cross pollination; see Darwin, *Origin of Species*.

3. Darwin, *Origin of Species*.

4. Lyman and O'Brien, "Direct Historical Approach," 303.

5. Malina, *Social Gospel of Jesus*.

shame to interpret micro-social interactions and ascertain possible public perceptions concerning a particular action or person. Equally, within the Mediterranean cultures, economic realities of subsistence farming produced particular social interpersonal relations such as reciprocity. Beyond being regarded as expressions of sharing or acts of kindness, reciprocity refers to cultural capital or investment that comes from sharing. In view of contextual situations of precarious survival, poor rainfall and diseases, reciprocity through small gifts makes the households share the little that they possess. Sharing is extending virtues of neighborliness and channel of gift exchange essential during difficult times. Similarly, social phenomena such as marriage were understood from the perspective of tightening kinship relations.[6] Since they are derived from observable contemporary culture, direct analogies have advantage of providing plausible interpretive data regarding the less known past.

It has been noted that several disadvantages are associated with using direct analogues. These challenges include: (i) giving the impression that the present culture is similar to the past less known culture and (ii) it does not account for the chances due to migration and multiculturalism. Cultures evolve and lose their original cultural identities and practices. For example, the historical experiences of colonialism across Africa, India, Australia, and America resulted in extermination of indigenous languages and practices of several societies and, consequently, what is currently known is very different from their predecessors. Similarly, due to political and social changes, the present cultures inhabiting the Mediterranean geography are not necessarily direct historical heirs of first-century Judaism or Greco-Roman culture. Thus to assume direct correlation is missing the consequences of time and historical occurrences that shape societies over time.

What are indirect analogues? These come from cultures without historical and geographical links. This raises the question concerning the use of comparative analogues from cultures that are geographically and historically distant from the culture being studies. We can answer this by looking at the discursive assumption of indirect analogue. It assumes that irrespective of geography, cultures that are at the same level of political, economic, and cultural development share comparative traits. For example, societies living in preindustrial contexts share similar traits, but these are different from societies in industrial contexts. Recently, because of revival of contextual and postmodern approaches to the studies of the Bible, several

---

6. Malina, *Social Gospel of Jesus*.

Jesus, the Best Capernaum Folk-Healer

African scholars were enthusiastic to realize that some cultural practices narrated in the Bible relate to their own African cultures. Thus, given this impetus, several studies exist that draw comparative cultural aspects from African societies to those found in the Bible. To illustrate, literature by Laurent Magesa, *African Religion: The Moral Traditions of Abundant Life*, Jesse Mugambi, *The African Heritage and Contemporary Christianity*, and Kwame Bediako, *Jesus and the Gospel in Africa: History and Experience* start from assumptions of cultural continuity between African culture and some biblical cultures.[7]

From indirect analogue, African kinship practices, marriage practices of polygamy, peasant and subsistence livelihoods, and particular rites of passage such as birth and death rites are regarded as similar to those explained in the Bible. In addition, the practice of Levirate or *kinsman redeemer* marriage whereby the wife of the deceased is taken into custody by the male family members is common in Africa (Ruth 1:4). Among the Dondo people whom we shall discuss in detail, such practice is called *kugara nhaka*. It comes from the understanding that the wife is married to the household and the particular husband is mandated to give children on behalf of the household. This explains why, with support from relatives, *lobola* comes from the household father. Upon the news that his son has found a wife and with the help of other family members, the *paterfamilias* (the male head of a family or household) is responsible for raising the required *lobola*. Hence, in the unfortunate death of his son, after burial rituals are observed, the *paterfamilias* has the authority to decide who among his other sons or nephews can take care of the widow. A ritual is organized whereby all males within the household sit in a row at the courtyard. This is an important day for the widow and the household. She has to choose from the available males whom she wants to be her "kinsman redeemer." However, before the day, family members such as the aunties and others close to her would have whispered to her concerning the best choice. On the important day, she prepares food and water for handwashing and walks in front of available males and presents the food to her male choice. Behind the gesture of giving food and water to wash hands is a symbol of submission and agreement to exclusive conjugal rights. If the chosen male denies, he has to give a good reason to justify the refusal, otherwise he must accept the offer. If the reason given for the refusal is valid, the widow should then proceed to make

---

7. Mugambi, *African Heritage*; Magesa, *African Religion*; Bediako, *Jesus and the Gospel in Africa*.

her second choice. In cases where the widow is of age and her children are old enough to be able to look after her, she may opt to give water to one of her own sons, symbolizing that her own son shall take care of her.

In my view, discussions regarding "levirate marriages"[8] should be framed within limited-good societies. Within contexts of limited good, such practices function as economic and social security. Similar dynamics regarding "levirate marriages" in ancient Israel shows that such practices were for social and economic security. Marriages were performed toward the functionality of the households members and their welfare and not for individual right. Similarly, within precarious conditions due to draught and diseases and other adverse factors, polygamy is an acceptable practice in most African societies because it produces labor and improves survival chances of the household through food production. The more the children, the better the chances that some of them shall grow to adulthood. Equally, because it increases survival chances, in most Mediterranean societies, polygamy was a common practice. In addition, similarity in rites of passages such as birth, puberty, and death rituals exists between African societies and biblical cultures.

As an evaluation, direct and indirect analogues work the same way as comparative fits. In using direct or indirect analogues, the question is how the analogue assists in explaining dynamics existing in the past less-known society practices. Caution should be given that an analogue does not equate current occurrences to the past situation (A ≠ B). To do so, would be to run the risk of anachronism. Instead, without assuming compatibility in all aspects, the function of analogue A, is setting out questions around which we can understand B. Given this and assuming that analogues serve as comparative fits, there is no advantage of direct analogues over indirect models.

INDIRECT ANALOGUE OF THE DONDO NDAU PEOPLE OF SOUTHEASTERN ZIMBABWE

Brief History of the Ndau People

Most of the information concerning songs and poems performed to the chief and traditional healers within the community of the Dondo people

---

8. Or wife inheritance.

were collected during my trip to my village of the Dondo people of southeastern Chipinge district in Zimbabwe in September 2019. Three chiefs share the Ndau territory—Chief Mapungwana, Chief Ngorima, and Chief Musikavanhu. Being led by Chief Musikanhu, the Dondo people are one of the tribes among the Ndau tribes—Ngorima, Mapungwana, and Teve people. Although I migrated from Chipinge a few years back, I was born and raised among the Dondo people and there enjoyed most of my early adulthood. My frequent visits home to my mother and my extended family also provided me an opportunity to reconnect with my roots and reexperience my culture once more. Based on the above statements, I therefore regard myself as an insider participant observer.

Being an insider participant observer has its own advantages in that during my data collection period and while interacting with my data sources I already had a greater understanding of the Ndau culture, which enabled me to interact naturally with the data sources without hindering any social interaction. Additionally, the people I spoke to were more willing to discuss their cultural practices with me because they did not perceive me as an outsider who might misuse or judge the information they provided. Additionally, language issues were never a barrier in all those factors, assisted in shortening the time for my research as I did not have any obstacles prolonging my data collection.

My discussions with the people took the form of open-ended questions that, specifically, targeted the nature of songs and poems performed while visiting a traditional healer or chief and other forms of praise-giving. I gathered most material from the chief's family members such as Mbuya Dube and Ernest Mkwakwami who have first information concerning the events. After transcribing and organizing in interpretive variables, I complemented the data with written material from historians.

Elizabeth MacGonagle traces the history of Musikavanhu chiefdom from 1500 CE and notes that the Dondo dynasty is one of the several chiefdoms that, in the past, was vassal chiefdom under Mutapa kingdom.[9] Later as Mutapa lost control of the vast territory, several chiefdoms such as Ngorima, Teve, and Mapungwana began looking locally for their own security and trade. Thus, as early as the seventeenth century, the Ndau people traded among themselves and later with the Portuguese traders from Sofala and Beira. During this period, peace and tranquility prevailed in the region. However, the arrival of Nguni tribes that traveled north, running

---

9. MacGonagle, *Crafting Identity in Zimbabwe*, 41.

away from Shaka Zulu (leader of the Zulu kingdom in the 1800s) and in search of productive lands, changed the politics of the area. Nguni general Nxaba arrived first and settled in Sanga and began raiding local Ndau clans between 1820 until 1827. However, his stay was disrupted by the arrival of Soshangane in 1936 who established his capital at Mossurizi River. After pushing his rivalry, Nxaba migrated further north into regions known as Tanzania today, Soshangane established the Gaza state which extended into the Zambezi River in the north and borders the Swazi kingdom in the south. The oral history of Soshangane evokes bad memories among the Ndau people. It is told that Soshangane, unlike the Portuguese, disrespected the Dondo, all Ndau culture, and its ancestors. Before the arrival of the Nguni tribes, Chief Musikavanhu was a respected leader known for his spiritual abilities in rainmaking. Other chiefs as far as Matabeleland in the west and the Korekore people in the north, traveled to chief Musikavanhu for rain. However, Soshangane did not incorporate the Ndau culture and the important rain-making gods into his establishment. Instead, he proselytized everyone into Nguni culture through intermarriages. He sidelined many of the crucial Ndau cultural practices. In his attempt to defuse Ndau resistance, he took the Ndau's beautiful women, forced young boys into his military regiments, and killed Ndau men. After the death of Soshangane, his son, Mzila became king in 1884 and he continued the ruthless practices of his father over the Ndau people.[10] Mzila was replaced by Ngungunyana (1889) whose oral stories are still alive among most Ndau people. Ernest Mkwakwami whose father, Chief Musikavanhu of the Dondo clan, recalls, "*MaNguni aya akashata yaemho, akauraya tsika nemagariro edu*" (the Nguni people were very evil people; they disrupted our culture and way of life). Several chiefs were forced to be his vassal chiefs and those who refused were killed or excommunicated. Seeing himself as the only king, Soshangane introduced the system of *indunas*; local Nguni representatives that report directly to him.[11] Upon realizing their lack of cooperation, Chief Musikavanhu of the Dondo people and Chief Ngorima of Melseter were given death threats. In fear, they escaped west into Bikita, which is central of current map of Zimbabwe. They sought asylum in Bikita until Ngungunyana was displaced from the region by the Portuguese and the British who colonized Zimbabwe and Mozambique, respectively. On his departure, Ngungunyana took several Ndau women and some strong men

10. MacGonagle, *Crafting Identity in Zimbabwe*, 91.
11. MacGonagle, *Crafting Identity in Zimbabwe*, 91.

and relocated to Ihambane in the southern part of Mozambique where he later died. Elizabeth MacGonagle remarks that despite his political power, Ngungunyana did not win the hearts of the local people.[12]

Musikavanhu, whose name means "creator of people," rules one of the Ndau tribes; the Dondo people whose territory extend from the southeastern border of current Zimbabwe and Mozambique and share boundaries with Mapungwana in the east and Makoni in the west. Important about the Dondo people is their unique cultural tradition of art, gender role, knowledge of ethno medicine, art, and dance, which up to today, has not been severely affected by modernity and colonialism. Bodily tattoos (*pika*), colorful and attractive body incisions (*nyora*), and hairstyles set a Ndau woman apart from the rest. Importantly the people define themselves by their distinct Ndau language. In answering the Ndau identity, Enerst Mkwakwami remarked, "*TirimaNdau ngekureketa kwedu kwakasiyana neZeruru neamweni veshe*" (We are Ndau people and are known by our language which the Zezuru and other tribes cannot understand). Importantly he remarked, "*Tirivana veChiwarawara, vana veShondo*" (We are descendants from the great Serpent, the Penis).[13] The metaphor and designation "great serpent" or "penis" refer to a tradition that refers to the great chief as being shrewd and powerful.

Praise-Giving as Cultural Practice

Praise singing is a common traditional practice among Bantu and Nguni clans of Southern Africa and noticeable commonalities in the practice can be highlighted.[14] Also known as *izibongo*, praise-giving is an art whereby the praise-singer mentions the good deeds of a person, a chief, or local healer. The genre uses a mixture of songs and poetry that employs telegraphic language and metaphors. Etymologically, the term *izibongo* comes from the root verb *bonga*, meaning to thank, and is the same word used in reference to totems or clan names.[15] Comparative performances exist in the form of western *griot* of western Africa, who is a musician, performer,

---

12. MacGonagle, *Crafting Identity in Zimbabwe*, 41.

13. The symbol of "penis" as collective identity marker could be seen as identity marker derived from male physiology symbolizing power. To an outsider, it also indicates the patriarchal influence within the society.

14. Opland, "Structural Patterns," 96.

15. Kresse, "Izibongo," 172.

and storyteller. As we shall see with examples from the Dondo people, praise-giving is done at different levels—family or community level—and can be performed in reference to ordinary people at the household level or to a chief. As a genre, praise-giving makes the listeners vividly grasp the importance of the subject. To do so, the praise singer or narrator employs metaphors of animals such as lions, leopards, or eagles. Though the influence of Western culture should be acknowledged, praise poetry is alive in most African societies. Notably during initiation, boys are encouraged to recite their own praise poetry. The praise singer alludes to "lineage, physical and moral characteristics, and actions in the subject's public life."[16] The trick or training in praise-poetry is that at each instant of success, the praise singer should raise and pierce the sword to the ground while simultaneously chanting the victory. In some instance, instead of referring to oneself with real name, the metaphor of a lion or leopard is used which assists in painting a graphic picture concerning strength, feistiness, and prowess.[17]

Concerning delivery, praise poetry among the Bantu people, especially those which are done on public space, have been dominated by male performers. These utilize loud "guttural voices characteristic of traditional *imbongi*" and "breath units in the poetry with each line the equivalent of one breath."[18] In most cases, the praise singer sings issues that pertain to his community. By recounting history and presenting the urgency of the presence, he acts as point of reference concerning social consciousness, mediation, and reason. In him is the embodiment of an entertainer, a historian and conscience of society—telling the community things that transpired and raising consciousness about the present circumstances.[19] The performance is an intense public act that involves lots of gestures, movements, and voices; all brings the emotion associated with the performance. I concur with Russell Kaschula that "gestures therefore remains an important part of the performance and it is the performance as a whole which holds the audience attention."[20] In short, an *imbongi* is a performative art that employees a whole range of imperial gestures, tone, and mime to capture the mood and urgency of the presence.[21] No consensus exists regarding

16. Opland, "Structural Patterns," 94.
17. Kaschula, "Imbongi and Griot," 55.
18. Kaschula, "Imbongi in Profile," 68.
19. Kaschula, "Imbongi in Profile," 68.
20. Kaschula, "Imbongi in Profile," 68.
21. Kresse, "Izibongo," 175.

whether the praise singing in Southern African has discernible structure. However, agreement exists concerning features such as "intonation, pause and gesture."[22] In agreement with Opland and Kaschula, Kresse observes that succession of praise names are each followed by metaphors, forming "repetitive structures, such as alliterations and diverse forms of parallelism. In addition, each praise name is linked by extensive use of appositions, linking to a praise name, mostly at the end of a group of praises, a stanza, or a whole poem."[23]

To the Dondo clan, praise songs and poetry is a daily performance done within the household, in public and at festivals such as the installation of a new king.[24] Anthropologically, among the Dondo people, praise-giving toward an individual through songs or poetry is a form of encouragement to the receiver to continue doing what is culturally perceived as good.[25] Simultaneously, by streamlining what is culturally held as norm, praising the "doer of good deeds" would be an indirect way of prohibiting bad behavior. In the process, from seeing others being commended, the deviant character is compelled to emulate what is culturally considered good. In short, praise-giving is a cultural tool toward socialization or producing a "cultured person." From this, *imbogi*/praise-giving is a contextual poetic narrative intertwined with the culture and present needs of a community.[26] As a genre, praise singing is "rooted in the present, and readily respond to the context of the performance, expressing exaltation after battle, for example, gratitude at a gift, or grief for the dead as a funeral."[27]

Depending on the nature of accomplished virtuous deed, praise-giving can be short or long. Daily commendable chores within the household are usually short praise-giving characterized by a phrase or simple ululation. In addition, it is important to note that praise poetry and songs are not mutually exclusive. The praise singer may start with a song and then end with poetry; in between spectators may join in with various gestures such as ululating, clapping, and uncoordinated dancing or jumping. Being a community-acceptable way of according virtues, praise-giving may start with an individual but ends with the entire household joining the

22. Opland, "Structural Patterns," 96; Opland, *Xhosa Poets and Poetry*.
23. Opland, "Structural Patterns," 96; Opland, *Xhosa Poets and Poetry*.
24. Kaschula, "Imbongi in Profile," 68.
25. Kaschula, "Imbongi in Profile," 68.
26. Kaschula, "Imbongi in Profile," 68.
27. Opland, *Xhosa Poets and Poetry*, 85.

celebrations. For example, the mother may start chanting praise to the child and other family members joining in bestowing praise or singing.

Household Praise-Giving—Poems and Songs

As we already alluded, the household is the first site where praise and poetry is performed. Within the household children are commended for carrying chores such as fetching firewood, cleaning, and fetching water. Upon finishing the task, usually the mother chants a praise-giving poem. For example,

- *Mwaita mwaita Dube* (Thank you, thank you, thank you Dube)
- *Ujejeje ganda ravasikana* (You who adore the dazzling beautiful skin of young ladies)
- *Mazvimba kumba* (He who cannot stop giving)

Equally, the *paterfamilias* performs muscular tasks such as thatching or roofing the huts, building huts from wooden poles, and game hunting. Equally, upon return, the wife would briefly praise sing his totemic poem (*mutupo*). Usually totems are symbolized by an animal figure whose characteristics are projected as collective symbolic virtues of the clan. They function to distinguish clans and to avoid marriage within the same clan. Traditionally, upon being married, the wife is supposed to know the husband's family praise poetry. Equally, the husband is supposed to know the family poetry of his wife. In the event of giving birth and as expression of thanksgiving, the husband should recite her praise poetry and dance in her honor. As an important insight, among subsistence and peasant societies, praise-giving is a crucial way of encouraging one's gender role, identity, and skills. To illustrate, I have personal experience regarding the cultural practice of praise singing and poetry. During childhood, my brother Kumbirai and I would go and fetch firewood on behalf of the household or go hunt game meat. Upon return, my mother would recite our family totem, here translated into English by Smith:

> Thank you, Zebra,
> Adorned with your own stripes,
> Iridescent and glittering creature,
> Whose skin is as soft as girls' is;
> One on which the eye dwells all day,
> as on the solitary cow of a poor man;
> Creature that makes the forests beautiful,

Jesus, the Best Capernaum Folk-Healer

Weaver of lines
Who wear your skin for display,
Drawn with lines so clearly defined;
You who thread beads in patterns,
Dappled fish
Hatching round the neck of a pot;
Beauty spots cut to rise in a crescent on the forehead,
A patterned belt for the waist;
Light reflected,
Dazzling the eyes.
It is its own instinct, the Zebra's,
Adorned as if with strings of beads around the waist as women are;
Wild creature without anger or any grudge,
Lineage with a totem that is nowhere a stranger,
Line that stretches everywhere,
Owners of the land.[28]

Several aspects from the praise poem need an explanation. First, the act of praise singing from my mother identifies me by my clan symbol—the Zebra. Jeff Opland comments that names, as "nominal construction to traditions of praise poetry is characteristic of Shona praise poetry . . . names of forefathers of the clan, and of their sisters, abound in the praises, together with the names of the places where they are buried."[29] Most Nguni and Bantu families use animals as symbols to categorize their identity. Such practice was misunderstood by missionaries who mistook the practice as animism which is ascribing deity to animal.[30] Instead, as mentioned, totems were identity markers meant to prevent members of the clan from marrying within, which may cause genetic recession, thus, risking internal bodily deformities and stagnation of clan's numerical growth. Second, more than the visible act, praise-giving through song or poem demonstrates that the natural is intrinsically linked to the supernatural. Through praise-giving, my clan acknowledges that the ancestor is responsible for daily protection and is praised through clan praise-giving.

In addition to minor events, major life events such as birth or marriage are celebrated through poetry and singing. Dondo people are patriarchal and, therefore, the sex of the child is important. Though the mother is acknowledged, pregnancy and sex of the child is indicative of the

---

28. Dube, "Aretalogy of the Best Healer."
29. Opland, "Structural Patterns," 96.
30. Olupona, "Some Notes on Animal Symbolism," 3.

father's biological strength.³¹ He is the one that makes the woman pregnant through his power. A woman is regarded as passive recipient whose movement during sexual intercourse should be minimal lest she overpower the father and produce a female child. The child's sex is indicative of the father's performance during sex. For example, a male child signifies strength while a female child means the father was overpowered by the mother. This explains why, traditionally, most African men would not celebrate the birth of a female child because, her arrival is evaluation of his strength. Notably at childbirth, the male's clan poem is recited but also acknowledgment is given to maternal ancestry.

Most Dondo people request that the pregnant woman, especially at her first attempt, give birth at her father's house. Since giving birth is seen as being at a liminal space between life and death and the ancestors are responsible for making such decisions, thus, taking her to her paternal homestead is accepting that her ancestors would protect her during childbirth. During labor, skilled midwives or grandmothers perform the crucial job.³² The belief is that during childbirth, her family's ancestors would not allow childbirth complications or death of their own daughter. Thus, her paternal ancestor world protects her during the process of giving birth.

Consequently, upon successful childbirth, the husband's family must bring gifts and give praise to her ancestors for protection. For example, when my sister Charity was born, my father's family members brought some gifts that included few cloths for the baby and a goat to thank my grandmother. Upon arrival at my uncle's household, they began reciting my mother's family poem (*mutupo*). My mother comes from Mlambo Mkwakwami, Dziva totem and their animal is hippopotamus. Alternating between poems, songs, and dance, they celebrated my sister's arrival. Their performance and entry into the homestead lasted for more than fifteen minutes. Upon arrival at the center of the homestead, my uncle's family joined into the celebration. They exchanged praise-giving songs. At one moment, it was my father's ancestor and then later my mother's family ancestors. The visitors and neighbors who are not versed in singing the entire totem would come and only chant

> *Makorokoto Dviva* (Congratulations River)
> *The munaisi wemvura woyeeee* (The rainmarker)
> *zvaitwa, tatenda* (it's done, thank you)

31. Folkvord et al., "Male Infertility in Zimbabwe," 239.
32. Mutambirwa, "Pregnancy, Childbirth, Mother and Child Care," 275.

Jesus, the Best Capernaum Folk-Healer

Wakaramba kuwanda muroyi (only a witch refuses procreation).

Structurally, totemic names are a form of a formal address toward a respectable person. Importantly, praise-giving assumes that the ancestors are the real cause and recipients of the performance. Noticeable during such performances, women make the loudest ululations, clapping and dance. African women are performers of African rituals and culture through dance and music. During such performances, myths regarding the ancestors' power and exploits are told and celebrated; making praise-giving a myth-making episode. To ensure that the ancestors are happy and that the child belongs to the family, the nursing mother should breastfeed the baby in the presence of the in-law. If the child refuses and turns the head away from the nipple, then it is sign that the ancestors are not happy or that the child does not belong to the family. The Dondo people believe that children are innocent and ancestors speak through them. Such unfortunate occurrences are also interpreted as indicating that the nursing mother could be a witch and that she should confess. At the heart of such myths is the belief that ancestors are involved in bringing a child to the family and if the child is not of that family, they disapprove. Importantly, praise singing is a gendered performance which implicitly celebrates the productive vitality of the male side, the father's ancestors should approve an additional member to the family. Therefore, the ancestors have the final say in approving the celebrations.

In circumstances in which the mother confesses being a witch, then she should be held accountable by paying a fine to her husband's family. Stories are told of women who confess to having witchcraft or breastfeeding a snake. Some confess to having sex with "spiritual husbands" or dreaming having sex with another man. Others confess to waking up at night and digging up graves. A traditional healer (*sangoma*) may be called to ritually cleanse her before she is given permission to hold and breastfeed her own child. In the event that she confesses to be a witch, her family may be compelled to pay a token of apology in the form of a goat or sheep to be paid to her husband's family. The worst-case scenario is when she confesses that the baby belongs to another man or family. In such case, divorce proceedings may begin and her family is requested to pay back the *lobola* (bride money) that they received on the day of the consummation of the marriage.

Praise-Giving to the Chief

Chief Musikavanhu as the great chief of the Dondo people is praised at various community occasions. However, occasions such as the installation of a new chief are special occasions to observe how a chief is praised. The Dondo people believe that the chief is a direct descendent from the ancestor. Hence, the installation of a new chief is an endorsement of their continued presence and provisions throughout the village. Though invisible, the ancestors own the mountains, valleys and rivers. The entire land is a shared space between the living and the spiritual world. This is African concept of ecology. Through the chief, the ancestors oversees the peace of the entire territory. As the representative of the territorial ancestors, the chief is political, religious and social practitioner. Traditionally, he could institute punishment over people who steal, kill or violent territorial rules. Myths are told that at the installation of a new chief, miracles such as rainfall or other blessings from the ancestral world should happen. The occasion attended by other chiefs and traditional healers is spectacular. It is characterized by loud ululations and resounding clapping.

During the crucial installation process of a chief, the various sections of the village contribute various food items—beer, grain, and fruits. On arrival at the chief's courtyard, people sing and dance in praise of their new chief and the ancestors. The occasion is presided by the village traditional healer. Traditional societies such as the Dondo people function through two institutions, namely, *the chieftaincy* and *the traditional* healer institution. However, though a ritual practitioner, the chief relies on the powerful role of the traditional healer who mediates the community to the ancestors. Acting as an eye of the ancestors, the traditional healer is responsible for the morality and rituals of the community. Any deviation from the precepts of the ancestral world would result in calamity such as draught or famine. Acting in this role and upon hearing from the ancestors, the traditional healer warns the chief concerning any warning from the ancestral world. If it were a calamity that should be averted through rituals, the chief would announce community cleansing rituals.

During the installation of a new chief, adorned in animal skin and acting as curtain raiser who sets the tone and significance of the event, the skilled poet-singer (*imbongi*) stands in the middle of the courtyard and in a thunderous voice recites the chief's ancestry, family and great deeds. The attire of a lion or leopard skin is symbolic. It portrays the metaphors of power and invincibility.[33] The knob-kierie and shield made of animal skin symbolizes protection. Each chieftaincy has its skilled praise singer who through the years had perfected his skills and craft. As the poet recites, participants jump, clap, and make sounds in unison. In his recitation, the poet narrates the chief's genealogy, mentioning acts of benevolence. He may finish by highlighting the community's concerns and requesting the ancestor's protection and continued presence. A recent installation of Chief Musikavanhu is illustrative.[34] During the occasion, the praise poet sang,

> *Musikavanhu, Musikavanhu,*
> *Munaisi wemvura* (giver of rain)
> *Guramatunhu, woyee* (he who walks far distances)
> *Chiramba kusakara* (he who does not age)
> *Shumba inokuma kumatunhu* (the lion that has the loudest forest row)

Noticeably, the praise song streamlines the benevolence of the chief as a giver of rain. Equally, the chief's abilities of strength and power are highlighted. In his praise-giving, the history of the clan and the major events associated with the clan are highlighted. The ultimate purpose is revealing that the chieftaincy is divinely ordained and that, through the ancestors, the tribe had prevailed to its current form and status. The protective power of the chief is a very important aspect. A tribe whose chief is ritually unclean faced calamities or natural disasters of draught, pestilence, and diseases. An occurrence of such events is indicative of the anger from the spiritual world and the need for ritual cleansing and moral uprightness. Similar signals apply at a household level. Thus, a geographic area that is usually free of natural calamities and misfortunes is regarded as being at peace with the spiritual world and the chief of that area is praised. Equally, before inhabiting a particular area, people ask the moral nature and the condition of the area. If reports of natural disasters and lack of rain are known, then people avoid building their huts in such an areas.

Elizabeth MacGonagle refers to different practices by the Teve people in Mozambique whereby, instead of a once off occasion, the chief has routine praise singers at his courtyard. In reference to the Teve people, she remarks, "*Marombes* recited praises of the chiefs and performed with a group of dancers and musicians who played many-keyed instruments known as

---

33. Kaschula, "Imbongi in Profile," 68.
34. Interview conducted on September 27, 2019.

ambira made with iron, wood, and gourds."[35] In addition, under the Teve chiefdom, when people are accused of witchcraft, theft, of taking someone's wife, and the community wants to kill them by gouging eyes or cutting off limbs, these would run to the chief for refuge. Upon arrival, they sing and dance until the chief responds. She explains, "A large population of blind and maimed subjects stationed themselves at the doors of their 'kings and princes,' according to the report, where they sang, danced, and played instruments in exchange for sustenance from a gracious king."[36] That the chief is final arbitrator between the wrongdoer and the angry community indicates the extent of vigilantism among the Teve people. MacGonagle's study of the Teve people provides interested comparative insights.

While the Dondo people have high regard of their chief, they also hold their chief and ancestors accountable. This aspect has not been raised in most literature which only see ancestors as non-negotiating beings. During unfortunate events such as drought, pestilence, or outbreak of disease, instead of praising the chief or ancestors, the Dondo people would go to the chief's courtyard and sing songs of pleading. Since the chief is regarded as visible representative of ancestors, crying to him is also crying to great ancestors. Implied in the songs is the acknowledgment that the chief has power to stop drought and pestilence.

> *Mambo woye topera tose* (Chief we are perishing)
> *Woye woye, topara tose* (woye, woye, we are perishing)
> *Pepete, pepete* (perishing in great numbers)

Upon arrival and accepted into the chiefs courtyard, the chief is made aware of the arrival of visitors and is let known of their request. A courtyard is a large open space in the middle of several surrounding huts. The courtyard is sacred because that is where ancestor guard and hear the plea of the community. Here, the chief comes out of his hut and a mat is laid at the center of the courtyard where the chief would sit and receive all requests from the people. The chief is given a wooden plate and within it is tobacco powder. Ancestors receive food from the wooden plate, and tobacco powder signifies opening up of communication channels. In ordinary life, when two people meet, they exchange tobacco snuff as rituals of exchanging good will and friendship.

---

35. MacGonagle, *Crafting Identity in Zimbabwe*, 89.
36. MacGonagle, *Crafting Identity in Zimbabwe*, 89.

In the case of request of draught, specific songs which include vulgar language are sung and one of them is as follows:

> *Tinodegadwa mambo woye reupakacha ndiro kumashure* (we request for a water pond to bath our vaginas)
> *Tinodegadwa mambo woye reupakacha ndiro kumashure* (we request for a water pond to bath our vaginas)
> *Tinodegadwa mambo woye reupakacha ndiro kumashure* (we request for a water pond to bath our vaginas)

Interesting about rain request songs performed to the chief is the use of vulgar language. In the above song, the community women request the chief for rain to wash their private parts. The reason the request is performed by women is not clear. However, we can assume that, since women run household chores and, culturally, are supposed to be staying at home, the lack of water makes it difficult for them to perform their chores. In addition, the woman's body is sacred; it produces children for the ancestors. Hence, it should not be seen except by the husband who is given such responsibility by the ancestors. Singing vulgar songs is shaming the ancestors for not fulfilling their moral responsibilities. By parading naked bodies, the ancestors are supposed to feel agitated for letting their households down. The performance may last more than five hours of dancing and singing. During the procession, carrying beer pots, some women would lift up their skirt in full public view. Since the ritual is deemed sacred, young boys are not allowed to attend. Equally, men attend but they are not supposed to be in the same procession with women.

Later, the chief in company of elders of the village proceed into a shrine (*ngome*). This is a big circular sacred hut built for the ancestors. Here no one stays. In the hut, there are several clay pots full of *rapoko* (finger millet). A traditional meal for ancestors is made from *rapoko* and not maize meal. The flow of the hut is covered with animal skin. Here the chief takes the role similar to a high priest of presenting the people's petitions to the ancestors. He lays a small pot with beer and tobacco snuff and then evokes his ancestors, starting with the youngest until the eldest. Upon finishing, he comes out of the hut with an answer from the ancestors that their requests were heard. From there onward, celebrations continue through singing and drinking. If it is a request for rain, the chief would tell the people to quickly eat and rush home before the rivers flood. Mbuya Dube narrates, "Those days, our ancestors prayer for rain were effective. If they go into *Ngome* with request for rain, within few hours, it would surely rain. Even though

The Ndau's Dondo People as Indirect Analogue of Praise-Giving

the same rituals are still being done today but because of being ritually unclean, the ancestors, do not answer as they used to."[37]

Cultic Praise-Giving

We have already seen the importance of a community traditional healer working alongside the chief of the community. Beside the main traditional healer of the areas, the Dondo people have several other less popular healers who are approached daily concerning issues affecting the community. Different forms of praise songs are given to famous healers. Despite knowledge of Western medicine, the Dondo people treat traditional healers with great respect. A traditional healer is regarded as a mouthpiece of the ancestral world and they come in three categories—the herbalist, the diviner, and the lotcaster. A herbalist has knowledge of herbs. The diviner is a seer that uses the power of divination. Lastly, a lotcaster uses anointed objects to read the spiritual problem.

Concerning praise-giving, upon arriving at the homestead of the healer and while clapping hands, the visitor should recite the attributes of the healer. The clapping indicates respect; acknowledging that the healer's homestead is a sacred ground. While growing up, I observed several patients who frequented by grandfather's homestead for healing. Before arriving at his homestead, they removed shoes and organized their procession depending on age. The most senior person goes in front while the rest follow. Perhaps putting the eldest person in front is a way of informing the healer the extent of the gravity of their situation. While proceeding to the healer's courtyard, they should praise sing the healer's attributes. To my uncle, who was a healer, his attributes go like this:

> *Vanemukurumbira, tisvikewo pano* (You who is famous in the entire region, we seek your welcome)
> *Murapi wezvose* (Healer of all sorts of diseases)
> *Izwi remadzitateguru* (The voice of our ancestors)
> *Shumba, nemurwiri wevaranda* (The fearless lion and defender of the downtrodden)

As each attribute is being mentioned, the visitors clap and walk barefooted toward the shrine. The first line addresses the healer as one with fame and begging the healer for reception. Healers want to know that

---

37. Interview with Mbuya Dube, September 27, 2019.

people who come to them do so because of their fame and knowledge of their power. No healer wants to be approaches with a "trial and error" attitude. A comparative attribute is noticeable in Jesus of Nazareth who, in many cases, asks a patient if he/she believes that he can heal the sickness. Usually healers do not reject a patient seeking help. However, a healer can discern if a visitor does not trust him.

The call for the healer to welcome the patient and his/her entourage is an initial sign that the patient trusts the healer. The recognition is followed by a phrase that says, "*Murapi wezvose*" (healer of all kinds of diseases), which is an affirmation that the healer has power. The praise singers then proceed to say, "*Izwi ramadzitateguru*" (the voice of the ancestors), which acknowledges the healer as hierophany of the ancestral power. Lastly, the song labels the healer with metaphor of a lion, meaning that the healer has fame and power. Upon hearing the noise and commotion from outside, the healer signals the assistant to welcome the visitors and point them where to sit as they wait the healer to appear behind the curtain. The role of the assistant to the healer (*makumbi*) should not be minimized. It is him who interprets most instructions from the traditional healer and also further instructs the visitors regarding what they should do at each stage.

Upon being welcomed, the healer puts on his black colored cloth and holds an anointed cow tail (*hombore*) in hand. The *hombore* is anointed in traditional medicine and carries divine magic. The sick person is placed in front of the healer who then proceeds to smear oils on the patient. Using divination or lot casting, the evil spirit that causes illness is cast out.

Annually, most traditional healers organize celebratory festivals.[38] A majority of healers derive their powers through a sacred ritual known as *ukutwasa* or *kukamba*. Before going for the *ukhutwasa* ritual, the candidate may continuously fall sick. If no herbal solution is found, this may go sometimes until a traditional healer is consulted who would then confirm the calling from the ancestors.[39] In honoring their calling and replenishing spiritual power, healers take annual excursions by disappearing from community and spend time with the ancestors in the forest or shine. Similar stories from various African societies are told of traditional healers who disappear for spiritual replenishment. Though somewhat far-fetched, an African biblical reader may see Jesus' withdrawal as comparative motifs concerning divine healers. In one of Jesus' excursions, Mark reports, "And

---

38. Dube, "*Ukutwasa*"
39. Dube, "*Ukutwasa.*"

in the morning, a great while before day, he rose and went out to a lonely place, and there he prayed" (Mark 1:35).

Traditional healers from the Dondo people are known to disappear toward the season of crop harvest and return before the beginning of the new agricultural season (February until April). In the month of May, after harvest, people are usually resting and engaging in various cultural festivals of thanking the ancestors for the good harvest. This period coincides with traditional healers coming from their spiritual retreat and they join in the community celebrations. Upon return from isolation, usually, a healer would hold a celebration festival which has two functions: (i) to thank the ancestors for their healing powers and (ii) to celebrate their return from the spiritual world.

The second aspect is important because healers, if they misbehave, can be killed by the ancestors for abuse of power. Thus, the community regard the sangoma's absence from the village as the period of evaluation by the ancestors. During the period of absence, depending on performance, the ancestors may choose to increase the healer's power or terminate. Healers whose power have been increased are seen through their precise healing powers and predictions. Besides deriving powers from the ancestors or family spirits, some healers derive healing powers from "alien spirits." Within African cosmology, "alien spirits" are not enemies as the name may suggests. Instead, they are spirits from animals or other spiritual entities that can be tapped for particular purposes. For example, the spirit of a mermaid offers healing powers while the spirit of a baboon offers dance/entertainment and healing powers. The baboon spirit also offers athletic abilities which may make one win an Olympic medal.

During the celebrations, the healer invites relatives, neighbors, and fellow healers. Songs and dance are performed to celebrate the return of the healer and thank the ancestors or alien spirits for their healing powers. During the course of the celebrations, the healer may showcase his powers by healing people in attendance. Fellow healers with their particular powers and abilities may also showcase their powers. While growing up, I witnessed my uncle putting on his healing regalia and going into trance. Fellow healers and those in attendance would start clapping—coercing the spirit to manifest. Upon being possessed, he would start healing people and foretelling their problems and offering solutions.

Interesting to this study is both the songs and poems given to the healer in praise of his/her power. Most songs that are sung at such gatherings celebrate the healer for his powers and also the ancestors. The rhythm of songs is maintained through rhythmic clapping by the public and most songs are repetitions of a sentence or single stanza. For example, I recall the songs sung to celebrate my Uncle's healing power:

> *Murapi mukuru* (Greatest healer of all), (leader singer)
> *Uripano* (He is here) (the crowd response)
> *Murapi Mukuru weChipinge* (Greatest healer of Chipinge region) (leader singer)
> *Uripano* (He is here) (the crowd response)
> *Murapi anemukurumbira* (The healer whose fame goes far to the moon/to the valleys/ to foreign lands) (leader singer)
> *Uripano* (He is here) (the crowd response)
> *Murapi we zvirwe zvose* (The healer of all diseases) (leader singer)
> *Uripano* (He is here) (the crowd response)

As the rhythm continues and the intensity rises, indicating possession, the healer—(my uncle) would start groaning as he put on his healing regalia of red and black color. Upon noticing the possession, the crowd stands and claps louder while dancing. As the noise raptures and the dance becomes intense, to announce the arrival of the spirit, the voice of the healer would shout loudly. Noticeably, the choral song is meant to celebrate the healer and the gods, but also the region where the healer comes from. In the song, the healer is praised as best community healer who heals all forms of ailments. Mention is given concerning the healer's fame, his region and the nature of diseases he heals. Recounting such attributes is a way of praising the spiritual world for giving the community a healer of such nature. In addition, by repeating the phrase *"uripano"* (he is here), the crowd acknowledges the presence of the healer and the spirit. Healers are embodiments of the divine and their identity is queer. They possess the natural form as humans yet they are divine channels. The power embedded in their persona and clothing makes everything about the healer a fetish. In chapter 5, we shall notice how touching or talking to Jesus transfers healing powers.

Love Poetry

A brief discussion should be made regarding love songs and poetry among the Dondo. Traditionally, a young man would not simply approach a girl and say, "I love you." In most cases, usually the household father, in discussion with fellow village men, arranges the marriages in the absence of both the girl and the boy. Today, such traditional marriage arrangements have mutated into family members influencing their daughter or son but not directly involved in selection. Instead, upon meeting the woman of his choice, he was supposed to recite a love poem to the girl. Among the Dondo people, the water wells where women fetch water or paths where young women walk from fetching firewood are convenient dating sites. However, things are changing with the arrival of modern technologies such as cell phones and computers. Upon meeting the woman of choice, the man needs to seize the opportunity by expressing wit and exaggeration of personal achievements. One of the praise poems, goes,

> *Mwana akana ndidewo* (Beautiful lady, love me)
> *Chiso chako chinopenya kunge mwedzi wechirimo* (your face shines like summer moon)
> *Mazamo ako akamira kunge makomo* (your breasts stand firm like hills)
> *Mazino ako akachena kunge mukaka* (your teeth are white like milk)
> *Ukanyemwerera ndinopera simba* (when you smile, I am struck by your beauty).

Noticeably, the praise-song describes the lady's beauty using natural metaphors of moon, hills, and milk. In addition, the descriptions pay attentions to her body as attractive and fertile which speaks to the worldview that marriage is for procreation and a woman's physical beauty and fitness is indicative of her readiness to procreate. His performance through song should be accompanied by romantic gestures of helping the girl by carrying her firewood or water container. If she accepts the gesture, then the man has more time to walk with the woman and tell her his name, family name, and skills. Skills such as hunting, wood curving, and the ability to build thatched huts are signs that the young man has matured and is ready for marriage. Wit and the ability to tell funny stories is also an attractive skill. In traditional societies where modern entertainment equipment such as television and radio are limited, upon meeting at recreational areas for beer drinking, men entertain each other with hilarious stories. A person with skills to vividly tell a story with amusement attracts many friends. Such ability is called *nyambo*—a wit or a storyteller. Some even suggest that the skill is hereditary and people with such skill would not struggle to find a woman to marry. Today such a person is equivalent to a comedian.

Upon being persuaded, the woman arrives home where she tells her auntie or grandmother regarding the encounter. The elders would first evaluate the young man and his family to assess if there are no misfortunes associated with the family. If the household where the young man comes from is known for violence or shameful deeds such as murder or lack of economic status in the form of cattle or sheep, then the elders would advise to decline the proposal. However if the proposal is accepted and the household of the family has honor, then the request is escalated to the uncles and then the father of the woman. From that stage, the two families would start officiating the relationship and *lobola* negotiations.

CONTEMPORARY FORMS OF PRAISE-GIVING

Research by Russell Kaschula and Jeff Opland reveals that praise singing (*imbongi*) is a traditional practice that has evolved into current social spaces as a vehicle to convey current issues facing the community.[40] Both Kaschula and Opland regard the praise-singer (*imbongi*) as social-political commentator. For example, in South Africa, Bongani Sitole performs at crucial political gatherings such as during the Presidential National Address day and the inauguration of the new president. So far, except for Mandela, he has performed during the inauguration of all South African presidencies. Besides him, several other *imbongi* have performed similar roles during political rallies or crucial political gatherings. At such gatherings, the role of the praise singer is setting the tone by praising the national president for his role in tackling national issues. In addition, he shifts and takes the mediatory role for the people and sings concerning the people's suffering and issues which the president needs to hear. For example, he may sing about the water crisis, the frequent electricity load shedding and costs of living. Using contextual examples from the Zulu culture, Kai Kresse notes that praise singing has a dual task of criticizing and praising. Similar research carried out by Russell Kaschula with reference to M'Bana Diop, Bongani Sitole, Mbaye and Mkiva of West Africa and South Africa, noting their roles as political commentators and "prophets" to their respective societies.[41] Coming from the context of the people, the praise singer is well aware of the sentiments on the ground and, using this vantage privilege, if they are doing good, he praises the leaders. In doing so, he is

---

40. Opland, *Xhosa Poets and Poetry*; Kaschula, "Imbongi in Profile."
41. Kaschula and Diop, "Political Processes," 13.

The Ndau's Dondo People as Indirect Analogue of Praise-Giving

"reinforcing a feeling of public pride, strength and solidarity."[42] Yet if the leaders are distanced from the people, the praise singer uses his artistic skills through coded language to criticize the leaders.[43] Concerning this, Kresse comments, "*Izibongi* constitute a flexible tradition of interlinking art and politics in social life, based on the tradition of reason which is in itself flexible."[44] The *imbongi* maps the social experience or public opinion and, during his praise, presents it to the chief. In agreement with Archie Mafeje, Kresse comments that the regulative function of *imbongi* is to reconcile the personal leadership of the ruler with the people's will, and thereby the function of the bard is to interpret public opinion and to organize it.[45] In doing this role and by highlighting the needs of people, the praise-singer plays the crucial role of adviser to the chief.

Equally, the role of the *imbongi* as a critique of the leaders needs to be highlighted. Using direct or indirect commentary, the praise singer can take the role of analyzing the leaders for their abuse of power or being blind to the plight of the people. However, Russell Kaschula and Samba Diop caution that, sometimes where money and power is involved, proximity to political figures compromises the critical role played by imbongi.[46] Kresse comments that praise singing is a sacred art through which the performer takes the role of the ancestors who are the guardians of the village. Hence, in normal life, no man can criticize the chief, however the performance of *imbongi* gives "poetic license" to "transcend the particular in the interest of justice and truth."[47] Seemingly, as we shall see in chapter 3, the praise singer, truth teller and embodiment of the deity, is similar to Greco-Roman *paean* singers who were believed to be inspired by Mnemosyne—the god of memory, truth (*aletheia*), and justice.[48] To highlight similarities, Kresse notes, the imbongi performance is a "ritual licence" that, momentarily, permeates "rebellion," "revolution," and "obligation to truth."[49]

In addition, an *imbongi* or griot can function in highlighting people's social issues. During colonial times, the *imbongi* was tasked with keeping

---

42. Kresse, "Izibongo," 179.
43. Kresse, "Izibongo," 172.
44. Kresse, "Izibongo," 172.
45. Kresse, "Izibongo," 172.
46. Kaschula and Diop, "Political Processes," 22.
47. Kresse, "Izibongo," 183.
48. Burnett, *Art of Bacchylides*, 78.
49. Kresse, "Izibongo," 185.

Jesus, the Best Capernaum Folk-Healer

the memory of those imprisoned by the colonial regime and also keeping alive the cause of liberation. Examples of similar performances are found in Kenya and Zimbabwe where the music and poetry of Yali-Manisi or Chimurenga musicians such as Thomas Mapfumo, kept alive the Mau Mau or Chimurenga revolution, respectively.[50] Currently in South Africa, most *imbongi* perform social issues facing the people. For example, *imbongi* perform about the mining or worker's issues in general; focusing attention to the work condition and the low salary wages.

CONCLUSION

With focus on the Dondo people of southeast Zimbabwe, this chapter defines analogical method by taking note of several examples concerning the contexts and forms of praise-giving. Within the Dondo cosmology, any form of power, be it human or spiritual, is revered and respected. At the domestic space, praise-giving is a sign of respect and narrative of motivation to children. Importantly, underlying all domestic praise-giving is the truth that the ancestors are the ultimate enablers of all the achievements that we have. In the next chapter, we shall see this aspect resurfacing. Praise-giving toward the chief and the traditional healers recognizes the human involvement and sees the spiritual power behind all physical power. That human being are channels of spiritual power is the main theme that we shall explore in the next chapter that deals with praise-giving within Greco-Roman society.

---

50. Kaschula and Diop, "Political Processes," 16.

Chapter 3

Heroes and Gods as Direct Praise-Giving Analogue in Greco-Roman Society

INTRODUCTION

IN THE PREVIOUS CHAPTER, we noted the context and various forms of praise-giving among the Dondo people of the southeastern part of Zimbabwe. In chapter 2, we noticed that the gods (ancestors) are praised for their benevolent acts of providing rain and health to the people. This chapter, which looks into direct analogue through praise songs and poems given to Greek-Roman heroes, heroines, and gods, complements chapter 2 concerning praise-giving to the gods. In chapter 5, analogues raised in chapters 2 and 3 are then used as comparative interpretive tools to reconstruct events around the healing stories in Mark's gospel. Both the Dondo and Greco-Roman worldview fit John Pilch's description of personalistic worldview in that both contexts see the supernatural permeating the physical events. In Greco-Roman worldview, success and fortune of any kind was attributed to the goodwill of the gods. Hence, praising the gods was acknowledging their power in directing natural events and thanking them for their power and presence.[1] The gods were believed to be responsible for everything that happens in people's lives, such as food, good health, safety, and protection during a journey. Conversely, since the gods compete against each other over power and supremacy, the negative results from their divine competition result in either good or bad events in people's lives.

1. Pilch, *Healing in the New Testament*, 69.

Hence, although the gods were perceived as good, they were also viewed as the cause for a variety of negative life situations such as death, ill health, and various misfortunes.

Since the gods permeate all spheres of life, their celebration takes various forms and contexts such as households, shrines, and stadiums or theaters. Households were immediate contexts to get in touch with the gods and acknowledge them. Here, depending on need, each household may subscribe to any god(s) they want. Figurines of a god such as Artemis would be displayed in the house and, when necessary they become crucial vehicles of divine presence. This means that, unlike our ideas of a missionary religion that seeks to convert people, Greco-Roman people were raised in their religion and gods were chosen based on need. Another aspect that we shall see is that gods were also chosen based on class. For example, due to their life experiences that resonated with that of the adherents, Hermes and Serapis appealed mostly to lower class citizens. To them, the struggles in the mythical narratives of the god were regarded as sources of hope and assurance that, having gone through similar experiences, the god is capable of assisting.

In addition, local shrines of gods such as Asclepius, Apollo, Demeter, Zeus, or Artemis were busy venues from people coming to offer thanksgiving and make various request. Some gods such as Zeus, Apollo, and Asclepius had universal reach and therefore, their shrines were located in many sections of Greco-Roman society. As we shall see with Asclepius and Apollo, although major shrines were at Pergamum, they had several shrines at thermal hot springs across Palestine.[2] At these shrines, various forms of praise-giving were done such as choral odes, dance and poetry. In many cases such as at the Olympic Games,[3] victory odes, dance, and poetry were done. We can imagine that each day shrines were busy places from adherents coming from different sections of society visiting to offer thanksgiving or petitioning a god for health or fortune. For example, at Asclepius's shrine, visitors would approach the shrine in song and dance and those already at the shrine such as the priests and other visitors would join in the performance.[4] This echoes our discussion concerning the people who arrive at the Dondo chief in songs and would be joined by other groups, thus forming a large group with thunderous celebrations.

2. McCasland, "Asklepios Cult in Palestine."
3. Also known as Hellenic Games.
4. Edelstein and Edelstein, *Asclepius*.

Heroes and Gods as Direct Praise-Giving Analogue in Greco-Roman Society

Besides the Olympics, gods were celebrated during their calendrical festivals. For example, fertility gods such as Artemis and Dionysus were celebrated during particular periods of the year. During such times, the adherents honor them for their generosity through harvest, rain, and health. A point of caution should be made here that, unlike us, Greco-Romans celebrated several gods. Therefore, celebrating and going to a shrine of a particular god would not deter one from going to the next shrine. Greco-Romans believed that gods perform various social needs such as health, well-being, fortune, and many other needs. Thus, an individual, depending on need, had the liberty of ascribing to several gods.

Why was music and dance good for the gods? The old Greco-Roman prayer that says "as you did once, do now again" captures their understanding of the music and dance.[5] The Greco-Romans believed that music was introduced to the Olympian gods by Apollo, the god of the muse, thus praising the gods through music and dance was regarded as mimicking the gods. Anne Burnett remarks, "Choral songs could create an old event by means of mimicry and then, since the gestures of the multiple chorus still contained a bit of their primitive authority, the demonic force of the original moment could be danced into the present moment."[6] During such moments, ecstasy and frenzy were central characteristics of the celebrations.

PRAISE-GIVING AT THE PANHELLENIC GAMES

Panhellenic games were the most prestigious events to celebrate the gods and heroes. During the games, several poems and songs were sung in praise of the individual who would have won a medal.[7] The Greco-Romans did not see the victory as one's physical effort. Instead, to win competition was the will of the gods. This further explains the earlier point that, for the Greco-Romans, life was a shared platform with the gods. Unfortunately, many songs sung at such events got lost and only few written compositions survived. The name given to the songs is *victory odes* or *epinikon*. Each event had specific competitions and particular god(s) associated with an event. The prestigious game and their associated god(s) are as follows:

---

5. Burnett, *Art of Bacchylides*, 7.
6. Burnett, *Art of Bacchylides*, 7.
7. Campbell, *Golden Lyre*, viii.

- *First*, the Olympic Games, these were performed at Olympia to celebrate Zeus through music and athletics. In Greek mythology, Zeus is the supreme god of the Olympia and all gods of the Olympia give homage to him. He is one of the children of Cronus and Rhea and his siblings are Hestia, Hades, Poseidon, and Demeter. Through his sister Demeter, he sired his daughter, Persephone. With his second wife, Leto, he gave birth to Apollo and Artemis. His first wife, Hera, gave birth to Hebe, Hephaetus, and Ares.[8] He is also the father of Hermes and Aphrodite. From this, we get the impression that Greco-Roman gods had life of their own—they could marry, have children or even engage in fights. In addition, they could hold grudges and seek revenge. For example, Hera (Zeus's first wife) fought Leto (Zeus's second wife) and even plotted against the birth of Apollo. Important to this study is that celebrating the gods is participating in their lives and seeing one's life as intertwined with that of the gods. The Olympic Games were organized each fourth year and the winner received an olive wreath. In terms of origin, the Olympic Games began during the seventh century BCE until the fourth, when Theodosius who became Christian banned them and labeled them pagan. Important to mention is that the Olympic Games were considered the beginning of the New Greek calendar.[9]

- *Second*, were the Nemean Games and these were conducted at Nemea during the month of July after every two years. Similar to the Olympic Games they celebrated Zeus, but also Heracles, through music and athletics. The winner would walk away with a prize of wild celery.[10] Heracles, the son of Zeus, was a Roman god associated with masculinity, power, and strength. Though without know tomb, he was believed to be born as a demigod, a person born with supernatural powers, and some believed that his personage grew from myths associated with hunter-gatherer culture where a person is celebrated for their power and strength.

---

8. Stewart, "Pindaric 'Dikē' and the Temple of Zeus."
9. Nisetich, *Pindar's Victory Songs*, 4.
10. Nisetich, *Pindar's Victory Songs*.

- *Third*, done every second year or fourth year, the Greco-Romans celebrated the Isthmian Games conducted in Corinth. These celebrate Poseidon, the sea god and Zeus's brother, through music and athletics.[11]
- *Fourth*, were the Pythian Games that took place at Delphi to celebrate Apollo through music and athletics. Importantly, Delphi is the mysterious island where, after being rejected by different islands, Leto gave birth to Apollo. These were organized two years after the Olympics and the winner walked away with a laurel wreath.[12]

As mentioned, the Greco-Romans organized their year based on the Greek games. For example, the Olympics marked the *first year*, while the Nemean and Isthmian were performed during the different months of the *second year*. The Pythians were done during the *third year*, and then the Nemean and Isthmian were repeated in *year four*. In addition to the major events associated with each corresponding god, each games hosted various games such as chariot racing, wrestling, boxing, pankration, athletics, long jump, discus, and javelin.[13] Except for chariot racing, all events were performed while competitors were naked and the spectators would be entertained from viewing erotic bodies.[14] Discursively, besides celebrating the gods, plausibly, through entertainment, the games were an opportunity to parade the extent of Greco-Roman masculinity, by displaying discourses of valor and prowess. The implicit narrative is that the stronger and more masculine body wins while the weaker and disabled body loses. In all this, ideas of honor go hand-in-hand with cultural assumptions about power and valor.

Winning a medal at any of the Panhellenic games was regarded as the most prestigious accolade. To illustrate the extent of prestige, the winner was celebrated by the entire community and seen as a god. Here we should remind ourselves concerning the belief that one accumulates immortality through virtuous acts. At the games, the moment of winning was a life-changing time. Upon victory, the announcer shouts out the winner's name, and as the candidate advances to the podium to receive the crown from the judges, family or a hired victory ode singer leads the crowd into praise-giving songs. The medals were simply crowns of olive, laurel, or

11. Nisetich, *Pindar's Victory Songs*, 4.
12. Nisetich, *Pindar's Victory Songs*, 4.
13. Nisetich, *Pindar's Victory Songs*, 4.
14. Nisetich, *Pindar's Victory Songs*, 4.

parsley. However, the prestige from winning outweighs the nature of the gift received. Winning any of the competitions from the games resulted in the fame of the village where the winner came from and the god who brought about the victory. Concerning this, Ippokratis Kantizios remarks, "The ancient city treated its native victor as hero, because he brought not only prominence to itself and, by extension, to the entire community, but also a blessing, since his achievement took place in the context of worship of a god, as a result he was deemed worthy of certain important privileges, such as free meals at the city-hall (Prytaneion)."[15]

Important to our study is the events that took place from the point of winning onward. Upon receiving the award, the crowd erupts in chorus songs and dance. Most choral songs were known celebratory songs from the villages. However, depending on class and status, some competitors hire a poet or praise singer who praise-sang the winner. Victory odes were a form of genre that celebrates the winner by narrating the winner's ancestry, the fame of his place of birth, and other known and famous deeds associated with his ancestry or personal accomplishments.

Among such decorated poets of singers were Pindar, Bacchylides or Simonides, who prior to the event would have composed songs to praise the winner.[16] This means that before the competitions, the competitor or his families approached a poet to compose songs or poems in his honor. Using his own skills and experience, the singer would take what he knows about the competitor's family, village, and other achievements. The trick is to make the celebration a public parade given to the winner. Sometimes, since the event was also a form of entertainment, the praise singer would use comedy to evoke laughter and exaggerate the fame and achievement of the winner. In agreement, the crowd, especially those coming from the same village as the winner, celebrated by jumping and dancing. We can imagine the deafening atmosphere associated with loud cheers and ululation.[17]

Celebrations would leave the venue to the streets and the winner's home. Along the way, songs, dance, and wild flowers and leafs would be thrown at the winner. In addition depending on the venue, various types of dance were performed. To those who were celebrating, the victory is beyond the winner—it is the victory of the gods of the village or city where the winner comes from. In addition, spiritually and compared to all other

---

15. Kantzios, "Victory, Fame and Song," 109.
16. Nisetich, *Pindar's Victory Songs*, 4.
17. Nisetich, *Pindar's Victory Songs*, 4.

cities, it meant that the gods look favorably upon their city. Hence, the victory had profound spiritual meaning whereby the winner becomes the visible embodiment of the gods—he is a god. Those who listened to the victory choral songs would hear both the celebration of the winner and the gods.[18]

Upon arriving at the winner's homestead or courtyard, dance performances such as *sikinnis*, *geranos*, or stork dance, and/or pyrrhic were exhibited. Some songs and dance such as the *dithyramb* or *iobakchos* were wild and licentious.[19] Given that competitions were done naked and performing *dithyramb* or *iobakchos* dance the spectators would likely join in the nude party dance. It is not clear whether women danced naked together with men. However, since such dances were performed to celebrate the gods or mimic the gods, it is plausible to assume that both male and female would be nude while dancing. In addition, certain instruments such as the oboe, "barbitos, phormix or kithara" were used.[20]

Later, such performances would leave the winner's homestead to the city's public arena such as stadium.[21] It is possible that, upon attainment of victory and in liaison with the imperial representative of the city or village, an impromptu feast would be organized.[22] Most regions of the Roman Empire were ruled by the governor together with the local representatives. In the case of Capernaum, the Roman representative was Herod Antipas who would report to Pilate in Tiberius. Here we should understand that the presence of the imperial representative meant that the gods were custodians of the city, region, and the empire. Burnett remarks, "The victory ode decorated the city as well as the winning athlete and it could do so in practice by choosing a myth that enhanced the locality."[23] To illustrate, in praising a winning athlete, *Bacchylides* praised, saying, "Binding your fair head with flowers, because of victory, you built up glory for Athens and reputation for the Oenidae."[24] Burnett further says, "The fame of a city was made by the fame by its victors, and the present victory had the power not just of recalling but of vivifying past victories, thus causing the whole

---

18. Nisetich, *Pindar's Victory Songs*, 4.
19. Furley and Bremer, *Greek Hymns*, 33.
20. Furley and Bremer, *Greek Hymns*, 34.
21. Kantzios, "Victory, Fame and Song," 109.
22. Kantzios, "Victory, Fame and Song," 109.
23. Burnett, *Art of Bacchylides*, 50.
24. Burnett, *Art of Bacchylides*, 50.

history of the place to shine with fresh lustre."[25] The mentality behind all this is that the natural abilities of the winner were made possible by the gods. Without them, misfortunes could have struck the winner and thus curtail his abilities. Noticeably, in the victory odes, temporary blurring existed between the human and the divine since the victories of the god are visibly demonstrated through the natural. Thus in celebrating the winner, explicit reference is also made to the gods.

Another important dimension exists in connection with the celebrations of the gods. The Greco-Romans believed that a person's *arête* virtues should be spread through word of mouth because it is such fame *kleos* which brings him immortality from the oblivion of death. Virtue similar to the moon should radiant its light for all to see. This means that, upon death, the people would still evoke the memory of the dead through songs and poetry.[26] Through poetry and songs, the winner's immortality preserves. The Greco-Romans believed the god Mnemosyne is responsible for keeping and preserving the diseased from oblivion through truth and memory. Interestingly, the word *mnemonic*, meaning remembrance, is derived from the name of the god Mnemosyne, who was the daughter of Tatans Uranus. She is mother to nine muses: Calliope (epic poetry), Clio (history), Euterpe (music), Erato (lyric poetry), Melpomene (tragedy), Polyhymnia (hymns), Terpsichore (drama), Thalia (comedy) and Urania (astrology). The muses were concerned with arts and entertainment.[27] Through the muse, memory of the diseased was evoked through songs and poems. Consequently, among the Greco-Romans, people feared to be forgotten or having their memory lost into oblivion. Thus, through public statues, songs, and poems one's memory is kept (immortality) alive. Thus, in reciting epics and odes, poets and singers such as Pindar and Bacchylides were preservers of truth (and immortality) through their songs and performances. In preserving truth, their songs should reflect *Eletheia*, the god of truth, by avoiding lies, exaggeration, and blasphemy. However, as we have already noted, poets and victory odes singers exaggerate their content to amuse and expand the fame of their client.

Lastly, the effectiveness of the victory odes depended on the choice of myth around which the story is told. The evocation of the lives of the god(s) was crucial in bringing together the natural event closer to its mythical

---

25. Burnett, *Art of Bacchylides*, 50.
26. Burnett, *Art of Bacchylides*, 50.
27. Burnett, *Art of Bacchylides*, 50.

meaning. The purpose of the dance and the song was to distinguish it from the rest of the event—making it immortal and "indistinguishable from the sung commentary that accompanied acts of cults . . . imitated the sacred choruses in their dynamic employment of myth."[28] To do so, the performers needed to "reconstituted isolated scraps of mythical experiences to make them bear upon the present . . . all partook of the eternal *eletheia* that attached to the ceaselessly repeated myths."[29] This aspect is crucial as an important comparative narrative strategy of Mark in giving us the healing stories of Jesus. From this perspective, we are able to ask, how does Mark present the healing stories as stories infused by the divine presence of the Messiah?

SELECTED CHORAL ODES PERFORMERS

Let us start by looking at professional performers. As we have seen, these were hired by a patron to perform for a fee. Therefore, it means that, in addition to daily performances and calendrical performances by the local community, a rich patron, upon winning a trophy from any of the Hellenic games, hired a famous poet to celebrate his fame and that of the god. Regarding this, Furley and Bremer remark, "From the earliest period poets in Greek tended to be itinerant, moving from place to place to perform at religious festivals or in answer to a commission from a wealthy patron."[30] We are not sure whether all itinerant performers were paid for their performances. An analogue from the Dondo people whom we saw in the previous chapters shows that some performers may perform without charging a fee but gain social prestige from associating with a famous person. If this was the case, then Furley and Bremer's remark is true. It means that some performers would travel from shrine to shrine and perform without a fee. On the other hand, perhaps due to the quality of their talent, they might demand to earn a living from performing at shrines.

Performers such as Bacchylides and Pindar were some of the skilled performers who were hired to perform at shrines and during Hellenic games. Because of their fame, they traveled around with a group of singers called *komos*. During performances, the victory ode singer had the challenging task of striding between the natural and the sacred. He should

28. Burnett, *Art of Bacchylides*, 78.
29. Burnett, *Art of Bacchylides*, 78.
30. Furley and Bremer, *Greek Hymns*, 38.

praise the winner of the Hellenic games and yet simultaneously praise the gods. Burnett explains, "The epinician ode in consequence put pressure on the supernatural world, just as a *dithyramb* or a paean did. The strength of a man was hymned with tone and postures associated with the imminence of the divine, and this meant that the composer of such as ode was conscious of great power, but also of a strong tension between the matter and the manner of his song. He had to stretch a single web of praise between earth and heaven."[31] In Burnett's words, the victor becomes, as it were, a god; attributed words such as "obios" and "makarios" and the whole procession hinted at a "culpable deification of mortality."[32] Here, I highlight three names, Simonides of Ceos, Bacchylides, and Pinder, looking into their biography and compositional technique.

Simonides of Ceos

Born in 556 BCE and known for being the first poet to charge a fee for his services, Simonides was the first professional poet known to write victory odes at the Hellenic games.[33] Before him and except for short refrains by the famous Archilochus, no known *paean* existed. From Simonides we begin seeing lengthy victory odes in celebration of various winners. Later, his composition inspired his nephew Bacchylides, who composed many elaborate and lengthy *paeans*.[34] He also inspired Pindar, who became a fierce competitor of Bacchylides. In cementing his name in the history books, he composed several victory odes to winners at various Greek games.[35] His songs reflects his context during the Persian wars, Artemisum and Samis and, therefore, "contain themes of men's helplessness before fate, nature and the gods and of the fleetingness of life."[36]

---

31. Burnett, *Art of Bacchylides*, 38.
32. Burnett, *Art of Bacchylides*, 38.
33. Robbins, "Public Poetry," 221.
34. Felsenthal, *Language of Greek Choral Lyric*, 126.
35. Lattimore, *Greek Lyrics*, 53.
36. Felsenthal, *Language of Greek Choral Lyric*, 126.

Baccylides

He was Simonides's nephew and less known until 1897 when an Egyptian papyrus revealed the extent of his works and influence. Contemporary and rival of Pindar, he was famous for "charm, legacy, and fluidity." The competition between him and Pindar was so fierce that stories are told that each time he composed a poem or a song, students of Pindar would accuse him of imitating their master. Commenting on Bacchylides's song, Theseus Dive, Burnett observes that Bacchylides was talented in using vivid language and expressive gestures that paint the story to the onlookers. Comparatively, in chapter 2, among Bantu and Nguni choral and poetry performers, we see similar skills of ability to use gesture, poetic and metaphoric language to give vivid images and intensity. Similarly, Bacchylides's songs were meant to impact "sense of immediacy" with "insistence over motion"; calling the listeners to partake in the song through emotions.[37] Burnett remarks, "The singers use a series of violent verbs to revive the intensity of these floating gestures that can never play themselves out."[38] In 468 CE, Bacchylides sang in praise of Hieron of Syracuse after winning the chariot horse race. Previously, Hieron had already won three previous Pythian competitions, but wining the fourth title makes him a special person. However, Hieron's successes were associated with trickery. During the competition instead of using his own and due to riches, Hieron bought both the horse and chariot to compete. This means that he bought a horse that ran fast and a strong chariot. In a normal situation, there was nothing great and exemplary regarding Hieron. Despite a bad reputation as a cruel person to his community, in raising Hieron, Bacchylides was careful to decipher virtue from Hieron's performance. In doing so, as an artist, Bacchylides puts emphasis on how people can learn from the good deeds of others. Burnett beautifully explains, "With an idealism apparently undaunted, he searched as usual for virtue and the answering touch of god, and gracefully managed to find them, even in this somewhat tarnished victory."[39] In picking up the good virtue from Hieron's win, Bacchylides sang:

> Voices cried from the gathered crowd:
> "Ah, thrice-blessed the man
> Who holds as his portion from Zeus

---

37. Burnett, *Art of Bacchylides*, 23.
38. Burnett, *Art of Bacchylides*, 23.
39. Burnett, *Art of Bacchylides*, 66.

> The prize of broadest rule among Greeks
> And known not to hide his towered wealth
> In black-veiled shadow."[40]

Bacchylides praises Hieron's hard work and victory and because of this, the gods have blessed him. Burnett states correctly, "Hieron is thrice-blessed because he is victor, because his excessive power comes from Zeus, and because he knows the best way to treat his equally excessive wealth, he knows how to burnish his gold with pious good fortune."[41] In Bacchylides's praise, there is implicit reference of people refusing to celebrate Hieron because of his evil deeds. In convincing the crowd, Bacchylides pointed the people where it matters most; Hieron is a hard worker who earns his fame from persistence and love from the gods.

Pindar

We cannot understand Greek praise songs without reference to Pindar. Through him, we get a fuller impression regarding the form and content of the victory odes. Pindar was born in 518 in Thebes and had a career that spanned seventy-two years. Because of his great talent, rich people such as Sicilian dynasty Hieron and Theron who won the chariot race at Pytho in 490 BCE contracted him. Pindar praised both Hieron and Theron in Pythian 6.[42] We already noticed Bacchylides's praise of Hieron which came twenty years later after that of Pindar. Besides the possibility of non-availability of Pindar, this has two meanings: first, that the rich had the means to hire whomever they wished and that they would not stick to one person. Second, it means that, though famous for their trade, praise singers were at the mercy of the rich people like Hieron. If one does not praise him well, you may lose the fame associated with praising a famous and rich person such as Hieron. From the revenue received from performances, Pindar bought an estate in Thebes where he lived until his death. In addition, Pindar was known for his generosity of donating money and paying for statues of various gods such as that of Zeus at the temple of Ammon at Kadmeia, the statues of Zeus Ammon at Kyrene, the statue of Hermes

---

40. Burnett, *Art of Bacchylides*, 64.
41. Burnett, *Art of Bacchylides*, 64.
42. Nisetich, *Pindar's Victory Songs*, 7.

Heroes and Gods as Direct Praise-Giving Analogue in Greco-Roman Society

Argoraios at the market of Thebes. He also funded for the inauguration the cult of mother Dindymene by the river Dirke.[43]

As the skilled choral performer, Pindar praised several gods and people. Like Bacchylides, his songs included choral performers that were performed by dancers.[44] From 476 BCE until 488, Pindar performed fourteen Olympian odes. Furley and Bremer comment that "Pindar's poetry and life reveal a deep commitment to the cults of his polis and to the basic tenet of Greek religion that only the gods grant men success, health, wealth and artistic inspiration . . . Pindar's use of divine and heroic myth in his epinician was deeply rooted in the major cults of his home town."[45]

In Olympian 1, Pindar celebrates Hieron of Syracuse for winning two times the single horse race in 482 BCE and 478 BCE. Because of such excellence, Pindar praises, saying,

> Water is preeminent and gold, like a fire
> Burning in the night, outshines
> All possessions that magnify men's pride.
> But if, my soul, you yearn
> To celebrate great games,
> Look no further
> For another star
> Shinning through the deserted ether
> Brighter than the sun, or for a contest
> Mightier than Olympia.[46]

In the songs, Pindar describes Hieron as the best; outstanding performer without competition. However, just after celebrating his hero, Pindar quickly acknowledges that such victory would not have been possible without the divine assistance of Zeus, the great god. He sang, "Overwhelmed in his mind with desire and wept you on golden pares to Zeus's glorious palace on Olympus, at another time, Ganymede came also for the same passion in Zeus."[47]

In Olympian 2, Pindar celebrates Theron of Akragas for the winning horse chariot in 476 BCE and describes his fortune and victories in wars

---

43. Furley and Bremer, *Greek Hymns*, 186.
44. Nisetich, *Pindar's Victory Songs*, 7.
45. Furley and Bremer, *Greek Hymns*, 188.
46. Nisetich, *Pindar's Victory Songs*, 82.
47. Nisetich, *Pindar's Victory Songs*, 83.

and his tragedies. The ode explains the complexity of life due to experiences of glory and yet also happiness and tragedy. Pindar sang:

> And Theron must be proclaimed
> For his chariot victory—
> Theron, true host of strangers,
> Bulwark of Akragas, exalter of his ancestors
> Who suffers much
> To win their sacred home
> By the river, and they became the light of Sicily . . .
> But with good luck
> Oblivion may come, for malignant pain
> Perishes in noble joy, confounded whenever a fate from the gods
> raises happiness on high.[48]

CULTIC PRAISE-GIVING

From praising winners of the Hellenic games, let us move to praising of the gods. We have seen that, in addition to Hellenic games, daily, the gods were praised in households. Living in our modern world where people have agency or control over their lives, we may not fully understand the extent of influence that the gods had over the people. However, our indirect analogue of the Dondo people may shed light in explaining that, in societies with less advanced medical and technological knowledge, the gods run the show. John Pilch gave us the term "personalistic worldview" to explain that such cultures do not separate the realms of the gods from that of humans. Though unseen or seen in the form of heroes, the gods permeate all human existence.

Given this background and in acknowledgment of their infinite presence, festivals were organized to thank or ask them for favors. A good starting point is asking—how were the gods celebrated? It is unfortunate that history did not preserve most of the songs and dances performed at shrines. At various shrines, performers and praise singers were the common people whose worldview was intrinsically intertwined with the influence of the gods. For example, singers of traditional songs at Dionysus shrine were common women. Inscriptions exist concerning the patron thanking the various invitees for their performances. For example in the Homeric Hymn to Apollo, the written inscription asks Delian women to

---

48. Nisetich, *Pindar's Victory Songs*, 88.

Heroes and Gods as Direct Praise-Giving Analogue in Greco-Roman Society

thank all performers present and those to come.[49] This inscription suggests that young women and men were recruited to perform at various shrines. While some songs were specially composed by skilled choral odes singers such as Pindar, most songs and performances were common to the community. No particular or universal form of performances existed. Instead, each community improvised its own preference. However, it seems that particular gods favor certain types of dance. For example, Dionysius's performances were mostly done while naked and the same is true with fertility gods such as Artemis. For example, choral performances to Poseidon or Artemis, where performers would dance naked, and a group of naked girls or boys would join in the performance, cajoling the visitors to dance. Furley and Bremer remark, "The girls were not only paying tribute to the goddess through their choruses, they were also presenting themselves to the menfolk of the community in a favourable light."[50] Upon being aroused, several myths exist of "a girl snatched by a passionate man or god from Artermis' chorus-line."[51]

Furley and Bremer seem to suggest that most shrines were vibrant with choral singer and dancers. Various groups of visitors arrived at the shrine singing and dancing their chosen song. Furley and Bremer remark that most visitors to Apollo, Leto, or Artemis would "sing their hymns without any proper order or decorum."[52] In some instances, some would be dancing while others would be carrying items brought to the god. Upon arriving at the shrine, the procession would be met by other groups who would joined in the dance and music.

In the second century, we have examples that professional praise-singers such as Aelius Aristides or other skilled priests at the shrines had known traditions regarding praising the gods. In earlier years and in his book *Education of the Orator*, Greek poet Quintilian gave what became a universal guide regarding praising the gods and heroes. He instructed,

> In gods, we shall first venerate the majesty of their nature in general terms, and then the power of each individually and any inventions which have given useful service to mankind. Thus the power of Jupiter will be shown to consist in ruling all things, that of Mars in war, that of Neptune in his control of the sea. Similarly with

49. Furley and Bremer, *Greek Hymns*, 23.
50. Furley and Bremer, *Greek Hymns*, 23.
51. Furley and Bremer, *Greek Hymns*, 23.
52. Furley and Bremer, *Greek Hymns*, 30.

Jesus, the Best Capernaum Folk-Healer

inventions: Minerva has the arts, Mercury letters, Apollo medicine, Ceres corn, and Bacchus wine. Next come any actions that antiquity attributes to them; while honor is also added to gods by parentage (e.g. if one is the child of Jupiter), by age (as with those born of Chaos), and finally by their offspring (as Apollo and Diana lend honor to Latona). It is grounds for praise in some of them that they were born immortal, and in others that they achieved immortality by their virtues.[53]

Using the guide by Quintilian concerning how gods and heroes were praised, let us look into how selected gods were given praise.

PRAISE-GIVING TO APOLLO

Born on the famous Island of Delphi, god Apollo was the son of Zeus and Leto and his sister was Artemis. In Greco-Roman mythology, the son of Zeus and Leto, Apollo was one of the celebrated Olympian gods and most celebrations toward him were done at Delos and Delphi (Pythian games).[54] His sister is Artemis. Apollo was famous for many aspects such as healing, archery, poetry, medicine, muse, and poetry. At Delphi, Apollo was famous for his prophetic oracles. Aristonoos of Corinth celebrated Apollo's prophetic ability, saying, "You pursue the art of prophecy, o paian, o Apollo . . . with oracles and melodies chords on the lyre, o Apollo" (lines 10–15).[55] Equally, Athenaios's paean to Apollo celebrates him, saying, "Who utters infallible oracles to all humans, you who seized the prophetic tripod from its evil guardian" (lines 18–19).[56]

To illustrate, I demonstrate praise-giving to Apollo through Pindar's hymn and the paean from Aristonoos of Corinth. Pindar praised, saying:

> I shall remember and not forget Apollo, the far-darter,
> At whose coming the gods throughout the house of Zeus tremble;
> And they dart up as he comes closer—
> All of them—from their seats, when he stretches his splendid bow.[57]
> She unstrung the bow and closed the quiver;

---

53. Russell et al., *In Praise of Asclepius*, 34; Quintilian, *Orator's Education*.
54. Miller, *From Delos to Delphi*, ix.
55. Furley and Bremer, *Greek Hymns*, 119.
56. Furley and Bremer, *Greek Hymns*, 136.
57. Clay, *Politics of Olympus*, 19.

Heroes and Gods as Direct Praise-Giving Analogue in Greco-Roman Society

> And, having taken it in her hand, from his strong shoulder,
> She hung the bow on the column of his father's house,
> From a golden peg, but him she led and sat on a throne,
> Then his father offer him nectar in a golden goblet
> And drinks a toast to his dear son, and then
> The other gods sit down as might Leto rejoices. (lines 1–9)[58]

Noticeable is the father-son relations and the celebratory moods seen from Zeus and Leto. However, this does not hide away the terror that Apollo gives to the other gods. Clay rightly comments, "The hymn opens with a violent and dramatic scene that vividly portrays the terrifying power of Apollo through his effect on the gods assembled of Olympus."[59] In the hymn, Apollo was born to rule all men and all nature (lines 30–39). The power and terror of Apollo was known even before he was born from Delo's response to Leto's response to have the island be the birthplace of Apollo. In response, Delos responded with deep concern, saying, "They say that Apollo will be haughty and greatly lord over the immortal gods and the mortal men of the barley-bearing earth" (lines 68–69). Delos further expresses apprehension, saying:

> Thus I dreadfully fear in my heart and soul
> lest, when he first sees the light of the sun,
> scorning an island whose ground is rocky,
> he overturn me with his feet and push me into the deep sea.
> And there a great billow will incessantly flood me
> up to my highest peak, while he arrives at another land
> where it may please him to establish a temple and wooded groves.
> (lines 70–76)[60]

The hymn goes further to celebrates Apollo as the god that solves all the human challenges that other gods have failed to solve. The motif that the god is far greater than other gods is crucial in inviting adherents to the god by setting apart the power of the god. Further, Pindar sang,

> Hymn the ambrosial gifts that the gods enjoy, and the sorrows
> which men under the hands of the deathless gods ever suffer,
> living without understanding and helpless, nor are they ever

---

58. Clay, *Politics of Olympus*, 21.
59. Clay, *Politics of Olympus*, 19.
60. Clay, *Politics of Olympus*, 19.

able to find any cure for their death or defense against old age. (lines 190–94)[61]

That gods afflict the living with various afflictions is a recurrent theme in many Greco-Roman hymns. To solve this, individuals needed to consult spirit mediums or oracles such as that of Apollo to determine which god has inflicted them. In the hymn, Apollo is regarded as the god that dictates the course of affliction and is able to remove the affliction. The kindness or compassion of Apollo is narrated when he travels to Onchestos where upon seeing a horse with a broken limp, he fixes the leg and makes the horse well.

> Coming to Onchestos, the resplendent grove of Poseidon;
> there where a colt, new-broken, recovers his breath from the pain of
> drawing a beautiful chariot; though he is skillful, the driver
> leaps from the car-box and goes on his journey. (line 230)[62]

The human cruelty of abandoning the injured horse is contrasted to the care and love expressed by Apollo in healing the horse. In addition, Apollo performed the most dramatic rescue by appearing at sea to merchants who were experiencing shipwreck. Greco-Roman worldview determines the kind of god to follow by looking at a god's level of compassion. A god that does not care for the adherents would likely receive few followers. Equally, it was important for the adherents of a particular god to make known their god by testifying the kindness of their god. The swift response of Apollo to a possible shipwreck is additional evidence of his benevolence and expression of his power. In Greek mythology, sea is the domain of the underground god, Poseidon. For Apollo, his virtue of kindness extends to the manner he relates to other gods. In Aristonoos's paean to Apollo, he states, "So as gods know gratitude, you grant Athena pride of place at the threshold of your holy temple, O Apollo: you thank her for her kindness she showed long ago" (lines 25–29).[63]

> These, pursuing their commerce and profit, were now in a black ship
> making a voyage to sandy-soiled Pylos and seeking the people
> native to Pylos; but they were encountered by Phoibos Apollo;

---

61. Clay, *Politics of Olympus*, 19.
62. Clay, *Politics of Olympus*, 19.
63. Furley and Bremer, *Greek Hymns*, 120.

Heroes and Gods as Direct Praise-Giving Analogue in Greco-Roman Society

down on the sea he suddenly leapt, in his shape like a dolphin. (lines 394–400)[64]

From most of the hymns and poems, one attribute associated with Apollo is that of his strength or power. In Pindar's sixth paean performed by the Delphian young men, Pindar sang,

> The long-range archer god
> In the mortal body of Paris
> And straightaway put off
> The day of Ilion's capture
> By shackling the brutal son of Thetis,
> Sea-goddess of the blue-black hair
> To his death in battle, the trusty bulwark of the Achaeaens,
> What resistance Apollo showed pale-armed Hera pitting his inbending strenghth against her And Athena! Years of effort sooner Achilles would have captured Troy had Apollo not been watching. (lines 80–104)[65]

Second, I illustrate with Athenaios's paean to Apollo (128 BCE) that celebrates Apollo's power, saying,

> When you shot the twisting snackey shape with arrow until the beast, with gasp on hedious gasp, gave up the ghost. Likewise, the foreign horde of Gauls which brutally attacked this land perished in the wintery snowstorm, Hail, Son of Zeus. (lines 17–25)[66]

Furthermore, Limenios's paean and prosodion to Apollo celebrates his power, saying, "You killed the beast . . . a whistling from its den, then Apollo, you protected Earth's sacred navel, when a foreign army brought sacrilegious plunder to your wealthy seat of prophecy but perished in a storm of freezing rain."[67]

To summarize, Apollo is celebrated through reflecting upon his lineage as Zeus's son, his power, and love of muse. The theme of generosity and kindness is expressed alongside his power. The recurring sub-theme of Hera, who tried to stop Apollo's birth and also plotted to overthrow Zeus

---

64. Furley and Bremer, *Greek Hymns*, 120.
65. Furley and Bremer, *Greek Hymns*, 104.
66. Furley and Bremer, *Greek Hymns*, 136.
67. Furley and Bremer, *Greek Hymns*, 138.

by giving birth to another powerful rival son, underscores the recurring theme of betrayal and opposition against Apollo.[68]

ARETALOGY TO ASCLEPIUS

Another most celebrated god is Apollo's son Asclepius, who derived healing powers from his father, Apollo, and his grandfather, Zeus. In understanding, we shall also apply Quintilian's structure that looks into celebration of lineage, fame, and attributes. Concerning lineage, Asclepius was the son of Apollo with the human daughter of the Thessalian king Phlegyas. Earlier on in his life, Asclepius's gift of healing was noticeable.

Tradition says before moving to Epidaurus where the famous shrine is located, Asclepius's shrine was at Trikka in Thesaly.[69] Other shrines were found in Corinth, Pergamon and Athens. As we shall see in the next chapter, during the first century, several of his shrines were also found across Palestine in areas such as Hammath, Emmaus, the Sea of Galilee, Neapolis, Ascalon, Bethsaida, Magdala, and Bethsaida. At each shrine, evidence shows that Asclepius's shrine existed alongside that of his father, Apollo, and both were worshipped simultaneously. An inscription at the cult of Apollo Maleatas at Epidaurus testifies, "Not even in Thessalian Trikka would one go down into Asklepios' sanctuary and seek his favour if one had not first sacrificed on the sacred alter of Apollo Maleatas."[70] A prayer to Asclepius in Herodas (third century BCE) began with the statement, "We greet you, Lord Paian, who rule in Trikka and have founded lovely Kos and Epidauros!"[71]

Asclepius was famous from healing battle wounds from grey metal of stone missiles through applying herbs. At shrines, healing happens through a different format. The most common healing practice requires patients to sleep at the shrine and during the night and in a room shared with snakes, rats and owls, the patients receive dreams or see visions of Asclepius.[72] Instead of evoking fear, ghostly apparitions of Asclepius signify presence of divine power and healing. During such divine visitations, some received instant healing while others received their healing through instructions

---

68. Clay, *Politics of Olympus*, 36.
69. Furley and Bremer, *Greek Hymns*, 108.
70. Furley and Bremer, *Greek Hymns*, 229.
71. Furley and Bremer, *Greek Hymns*, 243.
72. Furley and Bremer, *Greek Hymns*, 208.

given in dreams. Those who received dreams consulted the priests for interpretation. The animals such as snakes and owls that rubbed themselves against the lying sick patients were believed to aid in transmitting divine healing. In addition to interpreting dreams, priest offered entertainment through choral music to the attendants.

I illustrate how Asclepius was praised through songs from Erythrai, Isyllos of Delphi, and Publius Aelius Aristides. First, the hymns sung by Erythrai (380–360 BCE) narrate Asclepius's genealogy, saying,

> Sing, lads of Paian famed for his cleverness, the farshooting son
> of Leto, Le Paian!, who fathered great delight for mortals, after
> he had lain in love with Koronis in the Phlegyeian land, le Paian!
> Asclepius, a god most famous, le Paian!
> From him, (i.e. Asclepius) were also born Machaon, Podaleirios,
> Iaso, Le Paian!, beautiful-faced Aigla, Panakkeai, the children of
> Epione, with glorious, bright Hygieia, Le Paian!, Asclepius, a
> god most famous, le Paian.
> Be pleased with me and approach our spacious city with
> gladness, le Paian and grant that we in delight see the welcome
> light of the sun with glorious bright Hygieia, Le Paian!, Asclepius,
> a god most famous, le Paian. (lines 1–15)[73]

Furthermore, Erythrai sings about Asclepius's kindness in healing diseases, saying:

> Leto . . . the defender, who once begot Asclepius, a healer of
> diseases and mortal woe, a vigorous lad, ie O Paian
> Whom throughout the Pelian peaks the Centaur taught all skill
> and knowledge that wards off pain from mortal. (lines 15–20)[74]

In the songs, Erythrai praises Asclepius for his healing power demonstrated in raising the dead person. Angered for seemingly demonstrating power which only he can exercise, Zeus sought to kill Asclepius. The rest of the song recounts Asclepius's healing abilities and kindness.

The second illustration comes from Isyllos of Delphi (ca. 278 BCE), who praised Apollo and Asclepius, saying, "Apollo called this child after his mother Aigla Asklepios, the healer of illnesses, giver of health, great boon to mankind, Hail Paian, hail Paian! Praise to you, Asklepios: foster

---

73. Furley and Bremer, *Greek Hymns*, 208.
74. Furley and Bremer, *Greek Hymns*, 206.

your native city Epidauros, grant radient health to our minds and bodies, O paian, paian!"[75]

In narratives that echoes those given to Jesus of Nazareth, Isyllos recounts that Asclepius arrived in Epidaurus and saved the Spartans, and healed his sick son. Isyllos recounts,

> When my son saw you he stretched out his hand to you and spoke an imploring word of address: "I do not enjoy the blessings of your gifts, Asklepios Paian, please have mercy on me!" And you spoke to me the following clear words: "Take courage. I will come to you in due course of time. You stay here as I ward off distaster from the Spartans, since they justly observed the oracles of Phoibos . . . Asklepios, and you saved them. They proclaimed that everyone was to welcome you as saviour in a holy feast, spreading the word throughout wide Lakonia. These events, o greatest of the gods, Isyllos recorded in honour of your greatness, Lord as is right and proper."[76]

To complement, an inscription believed to be composed by Makedonikos of Amphipolis in 1 BCE praised Asclepius as healer of all ailments and giver of life. Makedonikos composed the song with intention to be performed in Athens by a group of young Athenian men "as they carried suppliant branches of olive and laurel" to the alter of Asclepius.[77] In typical fashion, the song begins by praising Asclepius as descendent of Zeus and of Apollo, saying, "Praise the Delian son of Zeus of the fine quiver and silver bow with glad hearts and reverent voices—O Paian!" (line 1).[78] Importantly in the song, Asclepius is described as the best healer, by saying, "The saviour who once bore the healer of ailments and misery, the kindly youth god Ascklepios—O Paian . . . we salute you, Helper of men, most famous god—O Paian. Asklepios, grant that we who sing your wisdom may forever flourish in life accompanied by delightful health—O Paian" (lines 6, 16–18).[79]

Last illustration comes from Publius Aelius Aristides Theodorus who was born in 117 AD (died around 185) in Smyrna in Asia. Although of a later century from Jesus, Aristides's praise-giving adds important insights concerning methods and form of praise-giving to gods. Aristides was a

---

75. Furley and Bremer, *Greek Hymns*, 230.

76. Furley and Bremer, *Greek Hymns*, 230.

77. Furley and Bremer, *Greek Hymns*, 266.

78. Furley and Bremer, *Greek Hymns*, 266.

79. Furley and Bremer, *Greek Hymns*, 266.

naturally gifted poet who traveled across the empire delivering speeches to high-profile people. In 144 CE, he traveled to Rome but ill health forced him to come home where he received healing from Asclepius's shrine in Pergamum. After two years of recuperating at the shrine and learning healing methods, he received a vision from Asclepius who encouraged him to use his natural rhetorical and poetry skills to praise-sing the god.[80]

Consequently, through songs, Aristides composed various poems and songs in praise of Asclepius. In Hymn 42 (Orr 42); *Address to Asclepius*, Aristides poured out his heart in praising Asclepius. He starts by humbling himself as one that had received more favor from the god—perhaps a reference to how the god healed and restored his health. Though able to offer sacrifices and incense, Aristides thinks that his gift in oratory is the better vehicle through which he can express his gratitude.[81] He reiterates the fact that Asclepius comes from the lineage of Zeus and Apollo. Through Asclepius, healing has been provided in various centers. Aristides went into detail to describe the fame of Asclepius as famous healer. In lengthy detail that starts with his own testimony, he says,

> Some, both men and women, claim that limbs have developed on their bodies, by the god's provision, when their natural limbs had perished: they tell various stories, some by word of month, some by statement on their dedications: for me it was not a part of my body but the whole of it that he himself put together and made firm and gave me a gift . . . for many people—no one could say how many—he has taken away pain and discomfort and problems both of the day and of the night.[82]

Notable in the above claim is Aristides's reverence of Asclepius as healer of all kinds of disease. The claim is supported by testimonies from the people whose health was restored. Here, Aristides gives us the impression that Asclepius is the healer known by all. It is possible to assume that, after receiving healing, people left written inscriptions at the temple site. For Aristides, it is the endless number of people that testified about Asclepius's great help that makes him god par excellence. He remarks, "I have heard some say the god appeared to them and stretched out his hand to them while they were at sea and in trouble and others will say that they

---

80. Russell et al., *In Praise of Asclepius*, 5.
81. Russell et al., *In Praise of Asclepius*, 37.
82. Russell et al., *In Praise of Asclepius*, 48.

succeeded in some business by following the god's advice."[83] Asclepius has even given advice to boxers concerning how to knock down the opponent during a boxing match.

Aristides goes further to celebrate Asclepius's various healing methods—drinking "chalk, one hemlock, one should strip naked and take a cold bath . . . stopping catarrhs and chills by baths in rivers and sea."[84] Sometimes Asclepius would require those with difficulty in walking to force themselves to take long journeys and others to fast.

Aristides concluded his address to Asclepius by thanking the god for giving him the gift of oratory. Here we witness the same complexity that, while Aristides has the gift, it is ultimately the god that must be given the praise. Aristides acknowledged that, while Pindar was a great orator too, he out-performed him because his oratory comes from revelation and guidance from the great god Asclepius. Through this gift, Aristides boasts that he has received praise and had delivered speeches before the emperors.[85]

In Orr/Hymn 38, *The Sons of Asclepius*, Aristides praised Asclepius's sons—Podalirius and Machaon. He starts by alluding that the song came to him in dream and, being from the gods themselves he wondered whether his actual performance would please them. However, he consoled himself that since the god Asclepius is the originator of the song and had chosen Aristides to perform it, the god has already approved Aristides's performance.[86] Following the conventions of composing aretalogy, Aristides began by acknowledging that Asclepius is the son of Apollo; who was son to Zeus—thus the two sons, Podalirius and Machaon, came from noble lineage, combining the greatness of Zeus and that of Apollo. Due to having Apollo and grandfather, the sons learned the art of medicine from the best teacher, therefore did not need to go to school.[87] Aristides goes further to praise the blessedness of Delos where Apollo was born; previously a barren and hostile island but now rich in flora because one of the greatest gods was born there.

According to Aristides, Podalirius and Machaon's fame as healers surpass that of Egyptian healers. He remarks, "They put down the famous doctors of Egypt and made acts of beneficence the token of their race . . .

---

83. Russell et al., *In Praise of Asclepius*, 49.
84. Russell et al., *In Praise of Asclepius*, 49.
85. Russell et al., *In Praise of Asclepius*, 51.
86. Russell et al., *In Praise of Asclepius*, 31.
87. Russell et al., *In Praise of Asclepius*, 32.

filled everywhere with medicine."[88] Aristides also describes Hippocrates of being mere layman with limited medicine knowledge in comparison to "Asclepiadae... made as it were a nation that preserves the art through the line of blood."[89] In addition, according to Aristides, Heraclides could not compare to the sons of Asclepius because the later were scattered, no equal honor, and they all faced misfortunes. Aristides sang praise of the two sons of Asclepius, saying,

> By contrast, the descendants of Asclepius, beginning with Machaon and Podalirius, were a common source of security and salvation for all, preserving their ancestor's art as yet another identifying feature of their race. Their fortune too was worthy of their chosen purpose, they were not banished or driven to be suppliants in anyway, but survived untouched by misfortunes, enjoying to the end one brotherhood, one mind, and one fortune.[90]

Similar tribute to Asclepius's sons is found in prayer to Asclepius performed in Herodos in the third century BCE which says, "Brother healers of rampaging illnesses Podarleirios and Machaon, we greet you and all the gods who share your residence and goddesses, father Paieon Come quickly."[91]

In addition to the issue of fame, Aristides praised Asclepius and his sons for generosity. Aristides remarks, "Their knowledge and generosity spilled out far and wide and to all the cities of the Greeks and many regions of the barbarians it became, and still remains, a glory."[92] For Aristides, the generosity of Poderilius and Machaon stems from their fathers, Apollo and Asclepius. These "were of service to their cities... eradicate bodily diseases, but also healed the sicknesses of cities or rather prevented them from taking hold in the first place, saving their subjects from both evils by making their rule accord, with their art."[93] Noticeably, generosity is the main virtue of any god and an essential attribute that makes a god likable to people. In addition, Aristides wrote songs in praise of various gods such as Heracles, Dionysus, Asclepius, Zeus, Serapis, and Poseidon.[94]

88. Russell et al., *In Praise of Asclepius*, 33.
89. Russell et al., *In Praise of Asclepius*, 33.
90. Russell et al., *In Praise of Asclepius*, 35.
91. Furley and Bremer, *Greek Hymns*, 244.
92. Russell et al., *In Praise of Asclepius*, 33.
93. Russell et al., *In Praise of Asclepius*, 37.
94. Russell et al., *In Praise of Asclepius*, 33.

PRAISE-GIVING TO DEMETER

Being Zeus's sister and through whom Zeus gave birth to his daughter Persephone, Demeter was one of the important and central gods. That she was a female god is important to see how female gods were celebrated. Furthermore, during the past fifty years, the hymn to Demeter (god of vegetation and animals) is the only hymn that received full scholarly attention. The hymn narrates the agony of Demeter while searching for her daughter, who was stolen by Hades, the underworld god, and their final renewal. It is a story of divine loss and renewal.[95] The hymn is divided into three sections:

a) The abduction of Persephone and its revelation to Demeter
b) The sojourn of the goddess at Eleusis
c) The aftermath, including her return and reunion.[96]

The happy times between the mother (Demeter) and daughter (Persephone) were disrupted after Hades (god of underworld), Zeus's brother, noticed Persephone's beauty and, after receiving permission from Zeus, the father, snatched her as his wife. Arranged for the reasons of uniting the Olympians, the marriage cannot happen in a normal way since Zeus needed to keep it a secret and the groom was supposed to snatch away the bride. The hymn opens by identifying the main character, Demeter.

> I begin to sing of fair-tressed Demeter, awesome goddess
> Herself and her slender-ankled daughter, whom Aidoneus
> Carried off, but deep-thunder Zeus, the wide-seeing gave her,
> In the absence of Demeter of the golden rod and splendid fruit.[97]

Demeter's lack of knowledge regarding the arranged marriage and her unwillingness to give her daughter Persephone away are painful realities in the story. Due to the motherly pain instinct from missing her daughter, Demeter could not eat for nine days. Hectate, the god of the cave (between the earth and underground), relayed to Demeter that she heard Persephone's cry while being abducted by Hades. Furthermore, Helios (the god who sees all) revealed that Zeus gave her away as wife to Hades—the uncle. In pain, Demeter left the company of the gods and took shelter among the

---

95. Clay, *Politics of Olympus*, 202.
96. Clay, *Politics of Olympus*, 202.
97. Clay, *Politics of Olympus*, 209.

mortals.[98] She stays at Eleusis where in gratitude of the locals gave them agricultural gifts and she established her mysteries among them. In defiance to Zeus while at Eleusis, she adopted a mortal male child, Demophoon, the son of Metaneira, and transferred divinity to the mortals. Despite her mourning state, Demeter retains attributes of caring goddess. Hence in the song, she is celebrated for her love and care.

> So she nursed in the palace
> The splendid son of wise Celeus
> Demophoon, whom well-girdled Metaneira bore
> She began raising Demphoon as god by anointing him with ambrosia—a preservative and "inspire him with her own divine breath"
> No eating grain or nurse (on mother's milk)
> (by day) . . . Demeter . . .
> Anointed him with ambrosia as if he were the offspring of a god,
> Breathing down on him his sweetly and holding him in her bossom;
> But during the nights, she would hide him in the strength of fire
> Like a firebrand
> In secret from his own parents.[99]

The practice of "baptism by fire" was common practice signifying burning of mortality. Zeus thwarted Demeter's plan of making human beings into gods. However, Demeter devised another plan of famine which would result in humans unable to bring offerings to the gods. Clay comments,

> Now Demeter will exploit the weakness of humankind, its dependence on agriculture to sustain life, to bring the gods to their knees. For the gods too are not completely autonomous; they depend on mortals not, to be sure, for their lives, but for their *timai*.[100]

Zeus then sent Iris and then Hermes to persuade Demeter to come back to Olympus—a request which Demeter refused unless her daughter is returned. The song has an unfortunate twist of Persephone eating six pomegranate seeds, meaning that she should stay underground for six month. In response, Zeus made a deal that for six months Persephone would stay on earth and reunite with her mother. This translated into summer with vegetation, flowers, food, and sacrifice. However, for the other six months,

98. Clay, *Politics of Olympus*, 222.
99. Clay, *Politics of Olympus*, 238.
100. Clay, *Politics of Olympus*, 247.

which she will be underground, these translate into Demeter's sorrow and consequently winter and no food. The hymn heightens with the establishment of Eleusinian mysteries, which put female participants' experience of marriage and funeral rites.[101] In short, the hymn celebrates the mystery of life that comes from giving birth. Yet, it reminds us of death, as life comes from mortal bodies that experience death.

PRAISE-GIVING TO HERMES

I selected and included the Hymn to Hermes because it raises universal questions such as: how do we celebrate within the context of social and economic inequality? In Greek mythology and genealogy, Hermes is Zeus's son through his wife Maia, which makes him Apollo's brother. Regarding origin, Hermes is celebrated as Zeus's son and due to fear of persecution, he was born at night at an unknown location by Maia—as "swift messenger of the gods."[102]

When it comes to Hermes, we are perplexed concerning how such an unconventional god could be worshipped or given praise. Though considered a young god among the Olympians, some scholars consider Hermes as one of the pre-Greek gods; known through various titles such as "god of herdsmen, a fertility god with chthonic associations, a fire god, a wind god, the divine trickster and the god or the stone heap or marker."[103] His position as a young god should be understood from the perspective of his role as one who arrives when the Olympian structure is complete but offers the roles of "mediation between host of opposition: among them, inner/outer, gods/men, life/death and male/female."[104] Having arrived late at the Olympians, Hermes's relationship with other gods was strained, especially Apollo. This cosmological conflict was translated to the worshippers of Apollo at Delphi and the plebeian devotees of Hermes.[105]

> And then she bore a child of many turns, of wheedling wiles,
> O robber, a cattle rustler, a leader of dreams,
> One who keeps watch for night and lurks at gates, who would soon

---

101. Foley, *Singer of Tales in Performance*, xii.
102. Clay, *Politics of Olympus*, 103.
103. Clay, *Politics of Olympus*, 97.
104. Clay, *Politics of Olympus*, 99.
105. Clay, *Politics of Olympus*, 101.

Heroes and Gods as Direct Praise-Giving Analogue in Greco-Roman Society

Show forth famous deeds among immortal gods.[106]

The character of Hermes is that of one who is less trustworthy—persuasive, seductive, and, it is characteristically ambiguous and riddling, concealing, as much as revealing, and abounding in double and ulterior meanings.[107] Both in devising his scheme and as messenger, Hermes is praised for his swiftness:

> As when swift thoughts pierce through the breast
> Of man whom dense cares whirl about
> And then beam swirls from his eyes
> So did glorious Hermes devise both words and deed.[108]

Clay's comment is poignant in saying that praise-giving focuses on "Hermes's mental alertness, his restless powers of observation, a glance that swiftly lights on all relevant details and misses nothing of importance, and lightening—swift intelligence that cuts through all obstacles and impediments to reach its goals."[109] He is an inventor, a creator with endless creativity. As inventor, he transformed a tortoise into a lyre.[110] The characteristics of finding strategies of survival resonated with the plebeians who became his devout followers.

To illustrate his wit, in Greek mythology, Hermes stole his brother Apollo's cattle and while driving them to the bank of Alpheios he attempted to conceal their footprints by making them move to and from the same direction. On his way, he also met an old man and he attempted to "extract from him a vow of silence."[111] As a true sign of shrewdness and upon being caught, he protested and requested that the Olympians hear the case. Apollo charged him of theft but he turned the tables and wittingly defended himself as being young and accuses Apollo of using force. With his desire to be seen and recognized by the Olympians, he requested Zeus to protect the weak.[112] When Zeus noticed the shrewdness of the young brother, he asked the rival gods to help each other in looking for the lost cattle but also reconcile. When the cattle were recovered Apollo noticed that some were missing

---

106. Clay, *Politics of Olympus*, 101.
107. Clay, *Politics of Olympus*, 106.
108. Clay, *Politics of Olympus*, 107.
109. Clay, *Politics of Olympus*, 107.
110. Vergados, "*Homeric Hymn to Hermes*," 2.
111. Vergados, "*Homeric Hymn to Hermes*," 2.
112. Clay, *Politics of Olympus*, 136.

after having been killed and some used as sacrifice by Hermes. To avert the obvious anger from his brother, Hermes took a lyre and sang a *theogony* of all the gods which soothed Apollos's anger. The two gods eventually reconciled and Hermes was eventually accepted among the gods as messenger of the gods. The hymn closes with reconciliation between Hermes and his brother Apollo.

PRAISE-GIVING TO APHRODITE

The Hymn to Aphrodite celebrates the female body and love in general. Greek mythology describes Aphrodite as Zeus's daughter through Dione. However, queer to the modern listener from the song is that Zeus was sexually enticed to have sex with her. Because of its lack of link to a particular shrine and its seemingly secular nature, the hymn to Aphrodite is one of the most complex aretalogies. Unlike other hymns, that celebrates the birth of a particular god, the hymn to Aphrodite does not have birth narratives and does not end with the establishment of a shrine. Instead, it ends with the "partial diminution of power of the goddess."[113] The hymn recounts "Aphrodite's seduction of the mortal Anchises."[114] The singer introduces Aphrodite as universal goddess; one who exercise her power by means of seduction, persuasion, and deceit even to the strong. The song goes,

> Hidden are skilled Persuasion's keys
> To the holy rite of love
> Phoebus; and among gods and men alike, there is
> A sense of shame openly
> To obtain the bed of pleasure from the beginning
> Her power to seduce is great such that she even seduce the great god—Zeus.
> Furthermore, the singer recounts, saying:
> And she even led astray the mind of Zeus who takes pleasure in thunder,
> He who is the greatest and received the greatest honor
> Deceiving his compact wits whenever she wishes,
> Easily she caused him to mingle with mortal woman.[115]

---

113. Clay, *Politics of Olympus*, 155.
114. Clay, *Politics of Olympus*, 155.
115. Clay, *Politics of Olympus*, 163.

Despite the anger and disavowal from Hera, Zeus supports Aphrodite and even allows her to mingle with the god causing them to "bore mortal sons to the immortals."

PRAISE-GIVING TO SERAPIS AT DELOS

I included this praise to Serapis because of two reasons. First, the celebrations praise a god that originally came from Egypt and later become famous throughout the empire. Second, being an outsider god, similar to the plebeian's (low class) celebrations of Hermes, and celebrations to Serapis were associated with the poor. This tell us that some gods were common among the rich while others were associated with the poor.

Composed by Maiistas as a communal celebration, the song was supposed to be accompanied by a dance and choral singing. Within a context of segregation and exclusion, the hymn celebrates the victories of the poor and outsiders. The aretalogy draws the emotions of the adherents into Serapis's story of how the deity was brought from Memphis in Egypt by Apollonius I. Food, dance, and even sexual performances were done all in honor of the supreme deity—Serapis. It was a story of adversity replaced by victory.

The song retells the challenges faced in building the temple of the god. For a while, the image of Serapis was housed in temporary shelter until Apollonius's son, Demetrius, was troubled by this situation. However, because of opposition from Apollo's followers Demetrius could not build a temple for the sacred god Serapis. On an island that was mainly controlled by Apollo, building a temple to another god was seen as an insult to the followers of great Apollo. Apollonius II, Demetrius's son, received dream instructions regarding how to build the temple. Having won lawsuit against his adversary, Apollonius II succeeded in building a temple which led to thanking and reminding the god that he built the shrine as the god had instructed.[116]

Two festivals were associated with celebration of Serapis—Pharmuthi/Pachon, which was mainly associated with slaves and low class people—given this day to celebrate the god and thanking them for their service. The main festival was the festival of Khoiak which seems to be the official occasion associated with Pharaonic or Ptolemaic festival of Osiris.[117] During the performance as sign of public performance, libation in the form

116. Engelmann, *Delian Aretalogy*, 2.
117. Abdelwahed, "Two Festivals," 4.

of wine was poured and participants carried palm branches waved in the air during singing and dancing. Since Serapis's (who later was also associated or depicted as Isis and Helios Zeus) celebration was associated with fertility, erotic dance and sexual-related activities were done in honor of the sacred deity. During such extravagant activities, poets and composers such as Maiistas would take to the stage to lead the crowd in celebration through music and dance.

DESCRIPTIONS OF PRAISE-GIVING TO LIVING HOLY MEN

We finish this chapter by looking at a holy man who attracted fame and praise from the people. Though not associated with shrines that we saw with the previous gods, holy men such as Honi the Circle Drawer (65 BCE), Hannina Ben Dosa, and Appolonius of Tyana were celebrated for their divine deeds. For example, Mishnah Taanit 3:8 reports concerning Honi,

> Once they said to Honi the Circle-Drawer, "Pray that rain may fall."
> He answered, "Go out and bring in the Passover ovens [made of clay] that they be not softened." He prayed, but the rain did not fall. What did he do? He drew a circle and stood within it and said before God, "O Lord of the world, your children have turned their faces to me, for I am like a son of the house before you. I swear by your great name that I will not stir from here until you have pity on your children." Rain began falling drop by drop. He said, "Not for such rain have I prayed, but for rain that will fill the cisterns, pits, and caverns." It began to rain with violence. He said, "Not for such rain have I prayed, but for rain of goodwill, blessing, and graciousness." Then it rained in moderation, until the Israelites had to go up from Jerusalem to the Temple Mount because of the rain. They went to him and said, "Just as you prayed for the rain to come, so pray that it may go away!" He replied, "Go and see if the Stone of the Strayers has disappeared." Simeon ben Shetah sent to him, saying, "Had you not been Honi I would have pronounced a ban against you! But what shall I do to you? You importune God and he performs your will, like a son that importunes his father he performs his will. Of you the Scripture says, 'Let your father and your mother be glad, and let her that bore you rejoice.'" (Mishnah Taanit 3:8)

Heroes and Gods as Direct Praise-Giving Analogue in Greco-Roman Society

To the Jews, making demands to God and drawing circles was regarded as magic, which to the Jews, should be condemned and the perpetrator excommunicated. However, even to the devout Jews they saw Honi's actions as similar to that of Moses; being close to God requested on behalf of the nation of Israel. However my interest in the story lies in the fact that, besides comparison to Jesus, scholars miss the fact that the same story talks about people coming to him.[118]

Equally, both Hanina and Apollonius were revered "men of God" whose lives are full of miraculous activities of healing people. However, the challenge we face is that most literature focuses on their individual personality and not the people around them. We do not have much information regarding how people come to them for healing and how they praised them for healing. My skepticism is affirmed by Baruch Bokser, who said that, to suit context and teachings, rabbinic literature changed the way the stories about Jewish miracle workers such as Hanina Ben Dosa were reported. Concerning Honi, rabbinic literature preferred presenting him as ideal image of piety.[119] In my view, Honi's story of making rain after three years of draught would fit in accounts where the healer received praise from the community for serving their lives. Besides the statement by the priest Shetah, one wonders how the people celebrated their wonder-making person.

CONCLUSION

In this chapter, we established that praise-giving varied in form and context. Because it attracted ordinary people, praise-giving to heroes was more spectacular and noisy. The celebrations began at the venue, to the streets, the homestead, and then to the public arena. Here, celebrations focused on the gods for giving ability to win during the competitions. In addition, we noticed that, being a personalistic worldview, gods received daily praise in the form of songs and offerings. Importantly, daily attendance by ordinary people made the shrines a busy place. In acknowledgment of the power of the god, people who arrived at the shrine in songs were greeted by others, making the celebrations loud and spectacular. In the previous chapter, we saw a similar atmosphere with the Ndau people whereby people visit the chief and sing until he comes out to address them. In addition, the chapter exposed us to choral hymns associated with each god and we noticed that

---

118. Achtemeier, "Gospel Miracle Tradition," 174; Goldin, "On Honi," 233.
119. Bokser, "Wonder-Working," 45.

gods were celebrated for their ancestry and for their various attributes of power and kindness. This is applicable to Apollo, Demeter, and Asclepius. Importantly we saw the intersection of praise-giving and class or status in that gods such as Hermes and Serapis were associated with the poor. In celebrating them, the poor resonated with the narrative associated with the god of adversity, hope, and triumph. We also notice the intersection of the variable to praise-giving and the female body where the god such as Aphrodite were celebrated for their sensuous qualities that arrested the gaze of many gods.

Chapter 4

Mark's Gospel and Jesus' Household as Site of Healing

INTRODUCTION

WITH REFERENCE TO THE Dondo of southeastern Zimbabwe and Greco-Roman society, respectively, the previous chapters 2 and 3 demonstrated forms and content of praise-giving. This chapter is the foundation toward chapter 5, where we shall plausibly interpret the Jesus healing stories in Mark's gospel as praise-giving performances toward Jesus. This chapter looks into the location of Mark's community, investigating the debate around its location. Furthermore, we zoom into the various social identities within Mark's community, asking the crucial question—who were the various social identities in Mark's Capernaum village. In addition, we look into the process concerning the formation of Mark's community, raising a question regarding social rapture and friction. Mark's community was both a social entity and a religious community that espoused particular beliefs regarding Jesus. How did its formation relate to important social institutions such as the various households led by the *paterfamilias* where its members came from? Importantly, in terms of its social organization, gender, and power, what were the noticeable internal structures that distinguish the group? Lastly, since the group presents Jesus as its healer and its missionary prop, what are the kind of sicknesses reported in Mark's gospel?

LOCATION OF MARK'S GOSPEL

Debate concerning the location of Mark's community focuses on three major possible locations: Rome, Syria, or Galilee. Support for Rome is based on several factors. Focusing on the theme of suffering and persecution that took place during Emperor Nero's reign (ca. 70 CE), scholars such as Mitchell, Collins, and Winn propose Rome as a possible location.[1] To support the argument, they say that

i) *first*, Latinisms such as reference to "legion" (Mark 5) and explanations regarding Jewish cultural and religious practices such as handwashing, point to a community that understood Roman imperial language and also geographically distanced from the Palestinian region;

ii) *second*, the persecution that occurred may have led to the death of the community's main leaders such as Peter and Paul, resulting in the community believing in an apocalyptic end of the world. Thus, as evidence, Mark chapter 13, the short apocalyptic text in Mark's gospel, indicates that the community believed that the world might come to an end soon. The description of violence and displacement indicated in the text should be regarded as prophecy after the event (vaticinium ex eventu) concerning events that the community was experiencing.[2] Furthermore, Ernest Best opines that such a traumatic situation had the potential of marking several people backslide. In response, Mark writes to encourage the community to "take up its cross" and follow Jesus. Taking the example of Jesus who suffered, Mark is encouraging his community to face persecution as their identity marker.

The other possible location is Antioch in Syria which is proposed based on the *modus operandi* of Jesus which is similar to that of itinerant preacher of that time. Howard Kee and Gerd Theissen proposes that, in Mark, Jesus is remembered as an itinerant preacher.[3] He calls his disciples to leave their household and join him in his itinerant lifestyle. During the first century in the region of Syria, several similar movements existed, thus making Syria a plausible location for Mark's community. Such movements believed that the world is coming to an end and that the life of purity and

---

1. Mitchell, "Patristic Counter-Evidence," 36; Collins and Attridge, *Mark*; Winn, *Purpose of Mark's Gospel*.
2. Best, *Following Jesus*; Best, *Temptation and the Passion*.
3. Kee, *Community of the New Age*; Theissen, *First Followers of Jesus*.

Mark's Gospel and Jesus' Household as Site of Healing

holiness is necessary. Similar models such as the Essenes were found in southeastern Palestine.

However, the growing interest over the social world behind the biblical narratives through the use of social scientific theories (archaeology, sociology, anthropology) by the Context Group,[4] tilts the discussion toward northern Galilee as a plausible location.[5] In agreement with scholars who suggest the region of Galilee as the most possible location, I shall further align my discussion with the views of Rene Baergen that sees Capernaum as its specific location.[6] This perspective is supported by the following arguments:

i) Mark's gospel gives supposedly firsthand information regarding the passion narratives which is plausible if such a community lived close to Palestine or got such information from Peter or any of the disciples that lived around Galilee.

ii) Furthermore, scholars that use narrative and space theory in reading Mark's gospel, perceive a clear narrative and contextual world of Galilee and surrounding areas. Concerning the narrative world of Mark, most of Jesus' narratives regarding welcoming people who were regarded as socially outcasts, such as the demon possessed, people with leprosy (Mark 1:40), and people with bodily defects, such as the woman with the flow of blood, took place in Galilee. In addition, the calling of the disciples and the formation of the Jesus community happened in Galilee (Mark 3:32–35). In connection to this, strategically, Mark's narrative sees Galilee as the place where the nascent Jesus movement starts.[7]

iii) Third, concerning the possible source material that came from Peter and Mary, certain information within the gospel came from a close circle of friends and relatives sympathetic to the Jesus movement staying in Galilee or Capernaum. Information such as the visits to the synagogue (1:27), the healing of Peter's mother-in-law, feeding and

---

4. Context group is a subgroup of biblical scholars that are interested in the social world of Jesus through the use of social science theories such as anthropology, sociology, and archaeology.

5. Theissen, *Gospels in Context*; Marxen, *Mark, the Evangelist*; Kelber, *Mark's Story of Jesus*.

6. Baergen, *Re-placing the Galilean Jesus*.

7. Van Eck, *Galilee and Jerusalem in Mark's Story of Jesus*.

sea-crossing stories, and passion narratives might have come from Mary or Peter. Such information circulated in Galilee and to early missionaries such as Paul who passed it to disciples such as Mark. Given that Mark, Matthew, Titus, and Barnabas lived and worked with Paul and to some extent, Peter in Antioch, it makes sense if the information become part of an oral tradition among early Christian households.[8]

CAPERNAUM VILLAGE AS LOCATION OF MARK'S COMMUNITY

Using arguments based on Mark's geography, Capernaum is touted as the village where Jesus started his movement. Located northeast of the Sea of Galilee, the village was geographically located close to the two major cities of Sepphoris and Tiberius. In addition, it was close to villages such as Cana, Nazareth, Migdal, Gadara, and Bethsaida. As a village, it had no significant or large infrastructure similar to those found in major cities. During Jesus' time, three significant items determine whether a place can be named a city. These are (i) infrastructural design in the form of theaters and stadiums, (ii) road pavement by stones was characteristic of a city, and (iii) whether the place had an imperial temple for emperor worship. The synagogue that was a Jewish community place of meeting and discussion concerning village matters and the torah was perhaps the only significant infrastructure in the village.

During his reign, Herod Antipas funded the building of two great cities of Sepphoris and Tiberius—a famous city and capital city, respectively. Sepphoris that was very close to Capernaum had many retired Roman officials and soldiers who had bought fertile lands in the region. However, one would expect constant reference to these great cities by Jesus. Alas, though Tiberius is mentioned in connection with the death of John the Baptist, no mention is given concerning Sepphoris in the gospels. However, recent studies by Jonathan Reed give a different suggestion by viewing Sepphoris as originally a Jewish village which was later taken over by the Romans who made it into a city.[9] Following this line of thinking, it implies that Mark's knowledge of the areas and surrounding villages is much earlier than later

---

8. Bauckham, *Gospels for All Christians*. Therefore, I find Richard Bauckham's suggestion that the Gospels were free-floating stories without specific context less convincing.

9. Reed, *Archaeology and the Galilean Jesus*, 97.

political developments that ushered in the building of Tiberius and Sepphoris. It further means that the Roman theater located in the city may be younger than Jesus' time. However, in my view, although an important argument, Jonathan's remark still does not account for the absence of Sepphoris given its importance and proximity to Capernaum. Given this, we remain with the same claim that, in Mark's gospel, Tiberius and Sepphoris are not given the fame they deserved as new imperial cities in the region. Why would Mark not mention such prestigious infrastructural developments that happened close to him? Several regions can be suggested.

Lack of mention of major cities in the region may speak to the tension that existed between villages and cities. The Jesus movement spread more in the villages and it regarded the cities as places characterized by imperial domination. Several factor contributed to this tension. First, cities were seen as places where imperial personnel such as governors and senators stayed. Thus, in terms of social outlook, cities represented the presence of the empire.[10] Second, landowners, known for displacing the peasants and taking their land, resided in cities, making cities the location of land-grabbers and oppression. The rise of taxation and tenancy was directly connected to the rise of cities.[11] Given this situation, it is plausible to argue that Mark could not have celebrated the rise of institutions that oppressed the villages such as Capernaum.[12] Jesus' message of commensality and hospitality suits followers that sought to strengthen kinship ethics and alternative livelihoods within a context characterized by land displacement and perennial droughts.

Concerning history, the village of Capernaum was established in 4 BCE and increased in population in the first century.[13] In terms of geography, lower Galilee, where Capernaum is located, was distinctly different from upper Galilee. Concerning terrain, the region is less mountainous compared to the north and boasts of trade routes that linked the east to the west. The valley of Beth Netofa and surrounding hill slopes were ideal places to cultivate vineyards and olive trees. Generally, the region was

---

10. Rajak, *Josephus*, 144.

11. Kloppenborg, *Tenants in the Vineyard*, 331; Oakman, *Jesus and the Peasants*, 13.

12. Zangenberg et al., *Religion, Ethnicity, and Identity*. An alternative view from Milton Moreland suggests that Jesus' itinerant lifestyle that calls out men to follow him and leave their gender role within the household, may not have been suitable for village livelihood (Moreland, "Galilean Response to the Earliest Christianity," 37).

13. De Luca, "Capernaum," 169.

characterized by "medium to high rainfall and a cold, humid climate."[14] Historians such as Flavius Josephus associate Capernaum with good fertile soils and beautiful sceneries. While there was natural beauty associated with the area, others have highlighted the issue of draught that was associated with the area. However, such natural calamities and in comparison to other villages in the area may not have minimized the natural conditions associated with the village.

We can add that the proximity of the village to the lake allowed for irrigation and better farming areas around the lake. In addition, fish transported to nearby cities such as Sepphoris and Tiberius in the north was one of the main businesses in the village. De Luca comments, "The stretch of coastline between Capernaum and the springs of Tabgha is particularly rich in fish even the twenty-first century thanks to the organoleptic characteristic of the spring water: warm, salty and rich in minerals. The fish are drawn here especially at night (cf. Luke 5:5) when the ambient temperature drops to 10°C."[15] Like most peasant communities, the Capernaum villagers survived on agriculture whereby a good harvest would be sufficient to carry them until the next agricultural season. Concerning this, fishery would provide much-needed protein to the households. To those with equipment and labor such as the Zebedee family, in addition to being protein supplement, fish was source of revenue from trade (Mark 3:17). Scholars who emphasize external factors affecting the city such as Richard Horsley and Ched Myers would view fishing as an occupation that arose within the village due to land displacement.[16] While it is true that the region was controlled by the Romans, villages such as Capernaum continued with their normal lives. Negative attitudes toward the established cities and their inhabitancy may have arisen, but, as K. C. Hanson points outs, the moral fibre and village lifestyle continued on the grassroots.[17] For more insight regarding such issues, K. C. Hanson's article "The Galilean Fishing Economy and the Jesus Tradition" gives important description regarding internal and external economic networks created by the fishing industry such as fishing families, hired laborers, taxation, processing, and markets in villages such as Capernaum.[18]

14. De Luca, "Capernaum," 169.
15. De Luca, "Capernaum," 169.
16. Myers, *Binding the Strong Man*.
17. Hanson and Oakman, *Palestine in the Time of Jesus*, 116.
18. Hanson, "Galilean Fishing Economy and the Jesus Tradition."

Mark's Gospel and Jesus' Household as Site of Healing

Jonathan Reed approximated the population of the village to be around one thousand people.[19] I suggest that the figure was even smaller, perhaps in the region of seven hundred to one thousand. In terms of local activities, being located at the banks of Lake Galilee, Hanson and Oakman opine that the village was famous for fishing and traders from neighboring cities traveled to the village and bargained the price of fish with local fisherman.[20] The story of Jesus whereby he calls his first disciples who were fishermen paints the picture of the area. In Mark 1:16–20, Mark reports that Jesus was walking along the banks of Lake Galilee when he met Simon Peter and his bother Andrew and later met James and John—the Zebedee brothers. Besides fishing, archaeological evidence of olive presses were discovered which suggests existence of agricultural activities within and around the village.[21]

Due to its frequency and comparing to other villages in the region, the Gospel of Mark presents the village of Capernaum as popular village (Mark 1:21; 2:1; 9:33). The frequency of Capernaum in the New Testament is second to that of Jerusalem, signifying its centrality to the ministry of Jesus and influence in the region. Scholars such as Rene Baergen have described Capernaum with various names, such as Jesus' "hub," "center," "headquarters," "constitutive of his career," and/or "emblematic for his kingdom."[22] Concerning this, Stepfano De Luca's remarks—"Capernaum figures as Jesus's stable domicile and the centre from which his Galilean activity radiates . . . towards the neighbouring territories of the Decapolis and Phoenicia"—sums up the importance of this village.[23] In this region, he performed several exorcisms and healed many. For example the healing of Simon's mother-in-law, the exorcism in the synagogue, the restoration of the man with leprosy, the healing of the woman with hemorrhage. The sea-crossing miracles that included feeding stories took place in this region. In several instances, Jesus would leave this region and travel north to Tyre and Sidon (Mark 7) or travel across the lake of Galilee into Ramot and Gamla but still he would come back to Capernaum, which obviously seems like his operation base. Christopher Zeichman, in an article titled "Capernaum: A Hub for the Historical Jesus," listed ten points to illustrate how Mark

---

19. Reed, *Archaeology and the Galilean Jesus*, 116.
20. Hanson and Oakman, *Palestine in the Time of Jesus*, 116.
21. Mattila, "Inner Village Life in Galilee," 312.
22. Baergen, *Re-placing the Galilean Jesus*.
23. De Luca, "Capernaum," 168.

redacted Capernaum as hub of Jesus' ministry. These are: inauguration of Jesus' ministry; authorizing the next generation of Christian ministry, returning here later; length of narrative devoted to Capernaum; gathering to Jesus in Capernaum, the site of Jesus' residence; Gennesret as "The Sea"; Capernaum as a "City"; and Capernaum as Markan innovation. Going through the ten points, Zeichman argues that Mark presents Capernaum as "locus for Christian and refuge."[24]

MARK'S GOSPEL AND SOCIAL IDENTITIES

Rene Baergen further postulates that the village of Capernaum had growing multiculturalism.[25] He remarks, "Encounter and interaction with the inhabitants of adjacent territories will have been particularly common."[26] A glance into the social characters mentioned throughout Mark's narrative indicates existence of the various social groups.

First, the existence of the centurion (ὁ κεντυρίων) who confessed concerning Jesus' divinity indicates cultural diversity in the village (Mark 15:39). In Mark's presentation of the centurion during Jesus' death, he is an ambivalent character. On one side, he confesses Jesus' divinity, saying, "This man truly was the Son of God!" A few verses later, possibly the same centurion is summoned by Pilate to confirm Jesus' death, which makes him an essential political organ of the Roman system (Mark 15:44). Matthew (8:5–13) and Luke (7:1–10), who seem to report a similar story as Mark, use the term Roman officer (ἑκατόνταρχος). Despite the different descriptions concerning identity, a common motif is that the centurion reported by Mark had a political network. Taking this perspective, we know that a centurion was a military leader of a group of one hudnred men. Comprising the group would be free men, mercenary soldiers, and slaves. Having his own army, he would be contracted by the empire to carry out security duties on behalf of the Roman Empire. With strong patronage links to Rome, governors such as Pilate, he was one of the powerful persons in the village. Since the village was located along the trade route, his duties were to ensure peace within the village and monitoring various types of people that come from the Decapolis and the eastern border. Citing the Rabbinic Tosefa Demai, Daniel Sperber thinks that the term *centurion* was used

---

24. Zeichmann, "Capernaum," 167.
25. Baergen, *Re-placing the Galilean Jesus*, 46.
26. Baergen, *Re-placing the Galilean Jesus*, 46.

interchangeably with the term *kitron*, who has the function, among others, of collecting tax. In Tosefa Demai, it says, "He who gives tax to the treasury gives to the *kitron* . . . first give the tithe and then give to him (*kitron*). The text differentiates tithe from tax which was supposed to be given to the *kitron*."[27] This may point to a mixed feeling in terms of relationships between the local villagers and the centurion as representative of the empire.

However, Mark presents the centurion in favorable light as the one who confesses the identity of Jesus to the community. In Mark 15:39 (see also Matt 27:54 and Luke 23:47) the centurion confirms to Pilate the governor that indeed Jesus had died. However, for Mark, it is his confession to the identity of Jesus as son of God that is important. Mark reports, "And when the centurion, who stood facing him, saw that in this way he breathed his last, he said, 'Truly this man was the Son of God!'" (Mark 15:39). The confession by the centurion confirms the existence and participation of various groups within Jesus' household. It may indicate that socially significant people such as the centurion had joined the Jesus movement and that people from afar had joined the household kingdom.

The second dominant social group with the village was the religious leaders—the scribes and the Pharisees. Though in his narrative Mark gives the impression that they traveled from Jerusalem to oppose Jesus, we can also assume a sizable number of religious groups in the village. At first, in Mark's narrative they seem to be concerned about Jesus' ability to abide by their religious instructions regarding obeying the Sabbath and food (Mark 2). The religious group—the Pharisees—seem to be in charge of the social life within the village. However, to Jesus the relationship was not collegial. Having witnessed Jesus violating the Sabbath day by healing a man with withered hand, they conspired with the Herodians regarding how to kill him (Mark 3:6). Herod Antipas had killed Jesus' mentor, John the Baptist, in Tiberius (Mark 6:14). Because of Jesus' link to John, the Herodians would give a listening ear to the Pharisees' plan to kill Jesus. Plausibly, the killing of John may have pushed Jesus to leave Tiberius in the south to Capernaum in the north—a less busy village with less imperial officials. Thus, though a religious group, the Pharisees would not mind exterminating characters such as Jesus and John who encroached into their socioreligious authority. In response to their authority, the relationship between Jesus and the religious leaders moved from cordial to severely strained. Jesus had no good

---

27. Sperber, "Centurion as a Tax-Collector," 186.

Jesus, the Best Capernaum Folk-Healer

words about them. He regarded them as hypocrites and socially insensitive group to the regional issues affecting the peasant.

In several instances, he denounced the way they interpreted and applied the torah as missing the core component of love and compassion. Mark 2:1—3:6, which narrates the tension over healing and working on Sabbath, demonstrates Jesus' care and compassion over the people vis-à-vis the religious leaders' insensitive hearts. In one of his several outbursts, Jesus condemned them, saying, "Beware of the scribes, who like to walk around in long robes and like greetings in the marketplaces and have the best seats in the synagogues and the places of honor at feasts, who devour widows' houses and for a pretense make long prayers. They will receive the greater condemnation" (Mark 12:38–40). Several social identity aspects can be gleaned from this passage. We are told that the religious leaders were visibly recognized by their regalia and were given public respect. They were given places of honor in synagogues and at feasts. Their lack of care and compassion was visible in the manner they treated widows. Eugene Boring poignantly comments, "Widows represents the vulnerable members of society, they had not inheritance rights in first-century Jewish culture, and most had to rely on family and community welfare programs. To ensure their well-being was the responsibility of community as a whole, specified in the Torah. Neglecting this responsibility was severely condemned by the prophets, since God was their ultimate advocate"[28]

A majority of the population within the village are labeled as the "crowd"—these were ordinary people that included farmers, artisans, and tradesmen such as fishermen. Mark gives the impression that the crowd was sympathetic to Jesus' teaching that they regarded as new and amazing (Mark 1:27). Besides teaching, they regarded Jesus as miracle worker who could heal their sick relatives. Some find his parables as stories of a sage (Mark 4). Some of them believed and followed Jesus and became part of the household.

To demonstrate their support for Jesus, they defended him against the plot by the religious leaders to kill him. In Mark chapter 12, Jesus challenged them and likened them to unconcerned vineyard tenants (Mark 12:1–11). Agitated by Jesus' remarks, Mark records, "And they were seeking to arrest him *but feared the people*, for they perceived that he had told the parable against them, so they left him and went away" (Mark 12:12). In this case, the parable of the wicked tenant had nothing to hide—the evil tenants are

---

28. Boring, *Mark*, 350–51.

the religious leaders who had failed in their obligation to look after Israel. This is the first time the religious leaders openly planned to arrest Jesus but they could not because they feared the rebellion from the crowd. By planning to arrest and kill Jesus, they lived up to their stereotype as murderers.[29] Here, the crowd believed in Jesus and protected Jesus from being killed by the religious leaders. However, having their hopes unfulfilled, they turned against Jesus during his arrest and crucifixion.

We can assume that existence of such varied groups indicates mutual coexistence of various groups—those who converse in Aramaic and those who speak Greek. We can equally talk about the affluent and yet also the poor—the slaves who resided in the village.[30]

SOCIAL TRAUMA DURING THE FORMATION OF THE HOUSEHOLD

Now that we established the context where Mark's community existed, we move to look at how it started. How was the Jesus household movement formed and what challenges accompanied its formation? That Jesus was fatherless and possibly homeless and shamed could be a clue to what happened to the Jesus movement soon after its establishment in Capernaum.[31] Within peasant and subsistence families, the continuous survival of the household depends on the male child. As carrier of the gene, the household father must have as many children as possible to ensure the survival and self-sustenance of the household. Two reasons for having many children are that, first, given the high mortality due to diseases, many children and women die during child labor. Therefore, giving birth to many children improves his chances of having children at old age. Second, within subsistence households, children are born primarily for labor and posterity. The more male children one has the more likely to have one's name survive. Girl children would be married and bring the much needed kinship ties. His girl children, while they also provide kinship ties, are an expense to him because of the amount of dowry required at their marriage.[32]

The above has implications concerning the social friction that occurred from Jesus' decision of leaving home. Having decided to leave

29. Evans, *Mark 8:27—16:20*, 239.
30. De Luca, "Capernaum," 171.
31. Van Aarde, *Fatherless in Galilee*.
32. Shelton, *As the Romans Did*.

Joseph's household and becoming itinerant preacher, such decision resulted in Jesus being disowned by Joseph for bringing shame to the family. A plausible explanation is that, given that Mark introduces Jesus as "the son of Mary" (ὁ τέκτων, ὁ υἱὸς τῆς Μαρίας, Mark 6:3) and not as the son of Joseph (οὐχ οὗτός ἐστιν ὁ τοῦ τέκτονος υἱός, Matt 13:55) may suggest that, by then, Joseph had died. Ancient Mediterranean families, being patriarchal families, were led by the *paterfamilias* who oversees the entire household. Under his control would be several family units of his sons who marry and live within the household. To his sons, he selects and decides type of bride he wants. To patriarchy, marriage is not for pleasure but for expansion of kinship relations, which is crucial during the times of need.

Commenting on the gravity of Jesus' decision, Halvor Moxnes remarks, "Jesus' break with his own family and his call to followers to do the same takes on a much more significant role than leaving home does in a modern and individualistic society."[33] By choosing to leave home, Jesus was disruptive and a sign of disregard to family values and kinship ties. He was a shame to the family, his village, and to himself. Mark gives clues regarding the challenges faced by the Jesus movement in establishing itself. At some point being convicted that God is calling him to an itinerant lifestyle, Jesus left the household, bringing shame to Joseph and loss of honor to himself.[34] Mark and other gospel writers, Matthew and Luke, record Jesus' brothers and sisters came out looking for him and accused him of being possessed by demons (Mark 3:21ff.). Mediterranean cultures believed that such behavior was caused by demon possession. Convinced that Jesus was demon possessed, his family members went out to take him back and convince him to reconsider his behavior. Mark reports, "Then he went home, and the crowd gathered again, so that they could not even eat. And when his family heard it, they went out to seize him, for they were saying, 'He is out of his mind'" (Mark 3:20–21).

Given that Mary and Jesus' brothers came out looking for him, it suggests their concern toward his welfare and their belief that such behavior is caused by demons. The accusation was a labeling tactic meant to restrain the deviant behavior back into the household.[35] However, interesting in the search is the absence of Joseph, who could be too embarrassed to look for his mentally unstable son or too old to be involved. The other possibility is

---

33. Moxnes, *Putting Jesus in His Place*, 151.
34. Moxnes, *Putting Jesus in His Place*, 151.
35. Neyrey and Malina, *Calling Jesus Names*.

that Joseph was dead. Whichever the case, the relationship between Jesus and his family was strained by Jesus seemingly abandoning his household responsibility.

Convinced by his calling from God, Jesus followed the itinerant preacher, John the Baptist, whom he followed, and then started his own ministry. Upon return, Jesus did not go back to his father's household, instead he settled in the village of Capernaum where he started preaching.[36] Out of the protection of the household, he was in liminal and vulnerable space. It is space characterized by shame and nonbeing. Within Mediterranean culture only slaves, the ostracized, and displaced persons occupy such position.

Mark does not give us reason why the Zebedee brothers (Mark 1:16) agree to follow Jesus. Given their status as fishermen and family responsibility, it is unthinkable why they agreed to follow Jesus. A reader who is aware of Mediterranean cultural values would agree with Mary Ann Beavis's remark that the first disciples' action of leaving their father with a hired servant is a shocking gesture, one that is unacceptable.[37] From a religious perspective, Eugene Boring noted that the story is unique in that it was not common for rabbis to call disciples. Such a practice was common with philosophers but not rabbis. Concerning the meaning of Jesus' call, Boring comments that Jesus' call of disciples implies that Jesus started the story of a community. He remarks, "From the beginning of the story is the story of a community, and there is no Christology apart from ecclesiology and discipleship."[38] We can deduce that Eugene Boring suggests the metanarrative significance of the story. His comment does not take away the apparent cultural disruption clearly suggested by the story.

However, important to this study is that Jesus called people who were at the periphery of society to form an alternative community. He also met people with leprosy—because of the condition of their skin, these were people whom society regarded as cursed by the gods. In the same category were every sick person, such the hemorrhaging woman. He also met travelers in the inns. Moxnes remarks that the Jesus movement was characterized by people in liminal condition; rejected by their households and yet found alternative fictive kinship family.[39]

---

36. Moxnes, *Putting Jesus in His Place*, 48.
37. Beavis, *Mark*, 48.
38. Boring, *Mark*, 57.
39. Moxnes, *Putting Jesus in His Place*, 151.

In several instances, Jesus gave statements that reflect being out of the protection of the household. For example in Mark 10:29, Peter raised concern about sustenance and provision of those who had left households to follow Jesus. In response, Jesus says,

> Truly, I say to you, there is no one who has left house or brothers or sisters or mother or father or children or lands, for my sake and for the gospel, who will not receive a hundredfold now in this time, houses and brothers and sisters and mothers and children and lands, with persecutions, and in the age to come eternal life. But many who are first will be last, and the last first. (Mark 19:29–31)

Equally a Q passage (Luke 9:57–62; Matt 8:20), reveals the tension in deciding to leave household and following Jesus. Luke reports,

> As they were going along the road, someone said to him, "I will follow you wherever you go." And Jesus said to him, "Foxes have holes, and birds of the air have nests, but the Son of Man has nowhere to lay his head." To another he said, "Follow me." But he said, "Lord, let me first go and bury my father." And Jesus said to him, "Leave the dead to bury their own dead. But as for you, go and proclaim the kingdom of God." Yet another said, "I will follow you, Lord, but let me first say farewell to those at my home." Jesus said to him, "No one who puts his hand to the plow and looks back is fit for the kingdom of God." (Luke 9:57–62)

Here we see two dynamics—some were prepared to leave their families and join Jesus in his itinerant ministry yet some saw leaving household as too much price to pay. To the undecided, Jesus called to the ultimate price or resolve. To one who was undecided, Jesus instructed that he should go and bury his father and then come and follow him (Luke 9:59; Matt 8:21). Such an instruction may sound too harsh and unsympathetic to a bereaved colleague. To those that believed, Jesus commanded them to preach the kingdom of God. However, there is clear family responsibility especially to the male followers of burying one's father and keeping one's household duties. To these, Jesus wanted resolve: they should go back or make up their minds to follow him. Jesus is calling for a radical break from patriarchal household; calling his followers to a no place; a liminal space. The metaphor of not looking back while one's hands are on the plough is calling to determination and resolve.[40]

---

40. Moxnes, *Putting Jesus in His Place*, 48.

Mark's Gospel and Jesus' Household as Site of Healing

Jesus declaring his followers a new household is the last phase in the formation of the household. In Luke 9:58, those who form a new household shall receive recompense; "hundredfold now in this time, houses and brothers and sisters and mothers and children and lands, with persecutions, and in the age to come eternal life." Mark is clear in saying that Jesus and the crowd moved into the household, signifying formation of alternative household and kingdom in contrast to the household led by the *paterfamilias*, the temple and Rome (Mark 3:31). Eugene Boring comments, "The house and the crowd are stock elements in Mark's narrative and carry theological freight."[41] Mark is using the house (see also 1:29; 2:1, 15) as metaphor for emerging household or institution vis-à-vis the temple and synagogue. By the end of chapter 3, we get clearer implication of Mark's household. The household was a radical break from the patriarchal household led by the father. Given that Jesus' own family remained outside the household suggests that joining the Jesus household formed new fictive ties of brothers, sisters, and mothers. Boring remarks, "The circle of his disciples had been constituted as new family . . . they belong to him as brother and sisters to the family of God (cf. Mark 10:28–30, Matthew 25:40, 28:10, Romans 8:29, John 20:17, Hebrew 2:11)."[42] Boring further explains, "That father is missing from this metaphor is not merely a matter of absence of Joseph from Markan narrative, but part of the theological imaginary: the family of God to which Jesus and his disciples belong can have many mothers, brothers and sisters, but only one father (cf. Mark 8:38, 11:25, 13:32, 14:36)."[43]

Robert Guelich concurs that the passage in Mark 3:21 calls for radical break from those who do not do the will of God from those who, like the disciples and the crowd, have separated from natural family to form a new family around Jesus.[44] The household comprised of people whose livelihoods has been dislocated from the patriarchal household. Jesus found them "in less formal structures, places: the agora in the town, the sea shore, the lake, the open road, mountain, and the wilderness . . . it appears to be a combination of people in marginal and liminal positions, typical of groups at *communitas stage* of group formation."[45] By forming such alternative

---

41. Boring, *Mark*, 106.
42. Boring, *Mark*, 110.
43. Boring, *Mark*, 110.
44. Guelich, *Mark 1—8:28*, 186.
45. Moxnes, *Putting Jesus in His Place*, 153.

Jesus, the Best Capernaum Folk-Healer

space, Jesus disrupted the household and village life. Jesus created place hospitality—restoration and healing.[46]

However, in Mark, the household faced perpetual persecution from the *paterfamilias* and religious leaders. Hostility from family members; even goes to the extent of being sold out to authorities (Mark 13:9–12).[47] Throughout Mark, the religious leader always suspected the Jesus movement of not abiding by the religious rituals and practices. Fear of disrupting imperial peace in the region, further puts the Jesus movement on Herod's radar as he sought to connive with the religious leaders to find fault that can convict Jesus of political insurrection (Mark 3:6).

RIVALRY HEALING SHRINES AND HOLY MEN AROUND CAPERNAUM

We now move to one of the subjects that is at the heart of our study—that is, besides Jesus, who were other healers and shrines found near or within the village. Did Mark know of rival healing shrines around the area or the region? At first, we need to correct the misconception that Palestine during the first century was closed to outside interference. Using evidence from archaeology, Jonathan Reed demonstrated the existence of trade links between inland cities such as Sepphoris and outside trade locations far east and even as far as Rome.[48] Through trade routes, religious practices associated with Apollo and Asclepius traveled into many sections of Palestine. Unlike our contemporary societies, during the first century, people had the liberty of attending various religions. As we noted in chapter 3, people followed a particular religion for practical reasons such as health, prosperity, and protection from misfortunes. I present the argument of Vernon McCasland and that of Megan Nutzman to explore the complexity concerning the existence of Asclepius alongside Jewish Christian religions.[49]

Although Asclepius's major shrines were in Pergamon, Epidaurus, and Kos, his shrines and those to his sons, Machaon and Podalirius, and daughter, Hygeia, and the worship of his father, Apollo, spread across the empire, including Palestine. Using archaeological findings, Vernon McCasland suggests that the cult of Asclepius worshipped alongside Apollo

---

46. Moxnes, *Putting Jesus in His Place*, 154.
47. Boring, *Mark*, 110.
48. Reed, *Archaeology and the Galilean Jesus*, 167.
49. McCasland, "Asklepios Cult," 221; Nutzman, "In This Holy Place," 281.

had shrines in Sidon, Tyre, and Palestine. In most places where the Greco-Roman gods spread, their worship was fused with local gods. For example, in Tyre, Asclepius and his daughter Hygeia were worshipped together with Eshmum—the Phoenician god of healing. Equally, worship of Asclepius or Hygeia was found in Sidon being named "Asclepius-Eshmun."[50] McCasland claims,

> It is reasonable to assume that this Phoenician cult of Asklepios-Eshmun was well known in Palestine as early as the first century. From ancient times there had been constant commercial and cultural relations between Phoenicia and Palestine. That this interchange was a commonplace in the first century is shown by the fact that Jesus and his disciples once retired into the borders of Tyre and Sidon. On that journey they must have passed near the temple of Asklepios at Sidon.[51]

In Palestine, Asclepius worship existed, various thermal baths were found in the region. The rift that extends from East Africa to Asia naturally created the thermal baths, among them being Emmaus-Nicopolis, Hammei-Ba'arah, Hammath Gaber, Hammei Livias, Hammath Pella, Hammath Tiberius, Killirhoe, and the waters of Asia.[52] Megan Nutzman's comment is worthy of consideration. She suggests, "Religious traditions coexisted at the baths before their ultimate Christianisation."[53] These miracle thermal springs were attended by Greeks, Romans, Jews, and Christians, and she further remarks, "What differentiated supplicants seeking miraculous cure was not the form of their cure, but rather the identity of their divine healer."[54]

Knowledge of Asclepius is evident from the hot springs at Tiberius, also known as Al Hammath or Hammath. Here excavations show close link between the synagogue at Tiberius and the hot baths.[55] Jews who took baths at the hot baths attributed the magical power to god. Later, in 99 CE, a coin was excavated whose inscription on one side was the image of Trajan and on the other the portrait of Hygeia, the daughter of Asclepius, suggesting that people of various beliefs attended the bath. On the coin, she is depicted

---

50. McCasland, "Asklepios Cult," 223.
51. McCasland, "Asklepios Cult," 223.
52. Nutzman, "In This Holy Place," 281.
53. Nutzman, "In This Holy Place," 281.
54. Nutzman, "In This Holy Place," 281.
55. Nutzman, "In This Holy Place," 281.

sitting on the rock with the waterfalls dropping on her, and on her hand the sacred serpent associated with Asclepius.[56]

Further east, in Gadara (known as Al Hammeh), a hot spring measuring 4600m^2 was famous for its healing magic from the times of ancient Israel; especially with stories such as that of Elisha who healed Naaman the Syrian of leprosy (2 Kgs 5:1–5).[57] Though Mark does not mention it, the Gospel of Luke mentions Jesus' visit to Emmaus and Bethsaida, small villages north of Jerusalem and perhaps much smaller than Capernaum (Luke 24:23, 28, 35). In the gospels, Jesus retreated to Bethsaida often and one of his disciples, Phillip, came from the village (John 1:44). From this insight, it seems Capernaum, Tiberius, Magdala, which were places frequented by Jesus, had bath shrines of Asclepius.

In John's gospel, at Bethesda, he healed a crippled man who, for a long period, was waiting for the magical sign for his healing (John 5:1–5). In an article, "Healing at the Pool of Bethesda: A Challenge to Asclepius?," Robin Thompson argues that acknowledgment of Asclepius, a popular healing god in Bethesda, changes the way we read Jesus' healing of the crippled man in Bethesda.[58] Taking a theological conclusion, Thompson argues, "The location of the healing serves as a challenge to the gentiles in John's audience: Jesus was more than a god who could heal—he was God who could provide eternal life."[59] I agree with Thompson concerning the narrative and rhetoric of John's story. However, the material culture in terms of several shrines across the empire proves that Asclepius was equally a powerful god. Therefore, while Thompson's theological conclusion is sound, it leans more toward privileging a christocentric reading of the story at the expense of a phenomenological or comparative approach.

ILLNESS AND SOCIAL DISLOCATION IN MARK'S NARRATIVE

Within the Jesus household that we shall deal with in detail in the next chapter, Jesus was praised as the best folk healer in the region. In this last section, we look at the social implication of the kind of sickness recorded in Mark's gospel. Within a personalistic and dyadic context, being sick had

56. McCasland, "Asklepios Cult," 225.
57. McCasland, "Asklepios Cult," 225.
58. Thompson, "Healing at the Pool of Bethesda," 65.
59. Thompson, "Healing at the Pool of Bethesda," 65.

social implications. A personalist worldview regards sickness from the perspective of the spiritual world. The term dyadic refers to a worldview whereby people define themselves from the perspective of others as opposed to individualistic worldviews. For Mark living in a dyadic society where social health depends on social interaction, sickness is social dislocation. Within this context, Mark does not report Jesus' healing in terms of etiology and cure that is characteristic of a biomedical approach. Instead, Mark is interested in the cultural and social implications of sickness. In his chapter "Healing in Mark," Pilch observes that Mark reports sicknesses from the perspective of gender and social implications.[60] Gender refers to the social roles that culture assigns to people based on their sex. Consequently, demon possession affects men's gender roles and Jesus exorcised them at community areas such as synagogues. Equally, at synagogues Jesus met men with withered hands and paralyzed limbs. On the other hand, fever, flow of blood, and other sicknesses are reported from the context of women's gender roles. Let us briefly look at four categories of sickness and their gender and social implication.

Social Dislocation Caused by Sickness Due to Evil Spirits

The first category of sickness reported by Mark is demon possession and this was reported from the perspective of gender performativity. Mark has three main reports of demon possession, found in (i) Mark 1:21, concerning the demon-possessed man in the synagogue, and (ii) that of the Gerasene demoniac in Mark 5:1–20; the last one being that of (iii) the story of the boy with the evil spirit in Mark 9:14–29. In addition, Mark refers to Jesus healing and exorcising demons from an unspecified number of people (1:39). To understand the social dislocation implied in the stories regarding demon possession, we need to understand the cultural expectations associated with men. Within patriarchal society, men were regarded as providers and sources of security to their communities and households. Consequently, the Gospel of Mark discusses demon possession in relation to men's ability to perform their gender roles.[61]

A person who exhibited signs of being mentally disturbed or doing socially unacceptable behavior such as stealing or prostitution were regarded

---

60. Pilch, *Healing in the New Testament*, 66.
61. Pilch, *Healing in the New Testament*, 66.

as going through spiritual torment.[62] This explains why conditions of demonic attack are described using terms such as "torment" to refer to the suffering that the victim is going through. Certain Jewish magical practices believe that fumigating smoke from fish lessens demonic attack. Since such magical practices would not work, demon-possessed people were left to wander in the streets, forests, and hills. For example, the demon-possessed man who met Jesus in the synagogue could have wandered to the community center by himself or that, out of care, his relatives knowing that synagogues were also healing centers, brought him there. A clear example is the Geneseret demoniac (Mark 5:1–20) who was alone, bruising himself with stones in the forest. Their condition signified social fracture in several ways. The family of the victim was seen as cursed and shamed. If no restoration was done, such a person may die and no proper burial would be given to them.

A comparative explanation could be found among the Dondo people of southeastern Zimbabwe. For them, a demon-possessed person is due to an evil spirit, either an avenging spirit (*ngozi*) from dead persons who come back and seek justice or due to evil people who cast bad spells over someone (*chiposwa*). When the village comes to know about such a condition, the family is described as having a dark spirit over them (*pane mhepo*). Kinship networks and other social exchanges such as intermarriages are limited for families with evil spirits. Since they are enduring spiritual punishment, no one is supposed to assist them with food or shelter. The villagers believe that helping such people may result in transference of their condition. Consequently, mentally ill persons are left to wonder and fend for themselves and, in many cases with no social network, they die alone.

Social Dislocation Due to Physical Disabilities

Equally, Mark reports physical disabilities from the perspective of men's gender roles. To illustrate, four examples can be given: (i) Jesus heals a paralytic man (Mark 2:1–12); (ii) the man with the withered hand (Mark 3:1–6); (iii) Jesus heals a deaf mute (Mark 7:31–37); and (iv) the healing of the blind man at Bethsaida (Mark 8:22–25). Similar to the discussion about the demon possession of men, the inability of men to perform their gender role affects their honor. During Jesus' time, a man's honor was derived from his ability to fulfill his gender roles. For example, a man who did not have

---

62. Preuss, *Biblical and Talmudic Medicine*, 15.

an arm or leg found it difficult to protect and feed his family. Equally, in addition to being unable to fulfill one's gender roles, being deaf or being blind affects one's chance of being married. However, here cultural dynamics regarding the levels of disability need to be noted. Being deaf was associated with lack of comprehension and lack of understanding, especially of the torah. On the other hand, by not having physical eyes, blind persons could hear and were sometimes associated with having inner insight, associated with a seer.

Social Dislocation Due to Fever, Hemorrhage Other Sicknesses

While demon possession is mostly associated with men and mostly reported as being outside the household (Mark 1:21; 5:20), fever and hemorrhage affect women's gender roles (Mark 1:29; 5:25). Hence, Mark narrates them as within the context of the household. As we noted earlier in this chapter, proximity to the lake of Galilee may have caused fever from cold or malaria, a common condition in locations such as Capernaum (1:29–31, 32–34). Given that within a personalistic worldview, sickness is caused by something that comes into someone's body (external), Jesus attended to Simon's mother-in-law in a similar way to casting out of demons.[63]

A comparative explanation from the Dondo people of eastern Zimbabwe may help. For the Dondo people, sickness such as flu is caused by *mhepo yakashata*, "bad air." Air can be ordinary and innocent but it can also be a carrier of evil spirits. This description comes from the belief that evil spirits are invisible and they travel through wind. In addition, since the air changes with seasons, certain spirits manifest themselves during certain times of the year. Lurking and invisible in the air, people innocently inhale with the air bad spirits that cause them to be sick. The Dondo people believe that the season of "bad air" is seen in the general sickness of children. Equally, such "bad air" affects women ability to fulfill their gender roles.

In addition, female-related conditions such as hemorrhage affect woman's ability to have children and perform gender roles (Mark 5:25–34). In peasant and subsistence societies, if identified around the domestic space, blood is good because it signifies fertility—the woman's ability to bear children. However, blood on the public space is danger; it signifies violence and death. A woman's start of her menstrual cycle was a crucial rite of passage that signifies fertility. Most women would be married at the

63. Guelich, *Mark 1—8:28*, 62.

young age of twelve. Although many died during child labor, the processes of marriage brought kinship ties that were crucial in extending channels of reciprocity. To the family that marries her, her ability to bear children adds to the growth of the clan.

A woman with flow of blood causes social dislocation at several points. The flow of blood was a shameful act by publicly humiliating herself as one that cannot fulfill her basic gender role of bearing children. In addition, her usefulness as a married woman who strengthens kinship ties was nonexistent. Furthermore, since she was considered ritually unclean, she could not perform her gender roles around the household.

A comparative interpretation among the Dondo shows similar dynamics and I have personal experience of a young woman from the village who experienced such condition. Consistent flow of blood is considered a taboo attributable to evil spirits. A woman that suffers from such a condition is taken back to her father's household with the request for the family to consult traditional healers to heal her. Her trauma would be in two parts—first, the community would shame her for returning from her husband's household. Second, given that she would not be in a position to bear children, her family may be requested to pay back the bride price or give replacement to the husband's family in the form of another young woman. Sometimes, agreement can be made between the two families to keep the marriage and allow the husband the choice of polygamy.

Mark also reports the sickness of Jairus's daughter (Mark 5:21–42) and that of the Syrophoenician woman's daughter (Mark 7:24–30). In terms of form, though they lack clearly known characteristics associated with exorcisms, they are reported as exorcism stories.[64] In both cases, to indicate that they relate to domestic gender roles, a woman is lying sick; meaning that she cannot perform her gender role. In the case of Jairus's daughter, his honor is equally involved because he is a man of social status. Within a dyadic culture, people frequented his household for advice. Women had various roles around the household of cleaning, cooking, nursing children and the elderly, gardening, knitting, and being involved in small-income crafts such as pottery. The elderly women were responsible for passing down the skills to the young. Hence being sick by a young women cut off the process of mentorship. In addition, it disrupts the process of division of labor.

---

64. Guelich, *Mark 1—8:28*, 382.

Social Dislocation Due to Leprosy

The last category of social dislocation comes from sicknesses that affect the skin. The Jewish health-care system associates skin disease with impurity and the victim should be cut off from society.[65] Several skin conditions such as skin rash or leprosy were seen as contagious conditions. Depending on severity, the victim was isolated or avoided. Mark narrates it as a condition that affected a man, but we can be sure that skin condition could affect both male and female (Mark 1:40–45). We can assume that Mark relates it from the perspective of male gender role because being away from the household meant that such households lost much-needed help around the household. As we have seen, men were responsible for all activities of protecting, providing, and manual labor. Though women work in the field as laborers, it was the man who, culturally, owns the land. Since land was inherited following the male line, his absence meant great social dislocation within the household.

CONCLUSION

This chapter began by investigating the possible location of Mark's community and settled for Galilee and Capernaum as the location. In terms of geography, surrounded by fertile soils, Capernaum was located north of the lake of Galilee. After following John the Baptist for some time, Jesus settled in this village and called his first disciples. Existing in a patriarchal society whereby, culturally, men are supposed to help with household chores of working in the field, providing, and protecting the household, Jesus' decision of leaving the household was perceived as a shameful decision. Equally, his disciples were shameful people. In response, the movement was labeled negatively to an extent of even planning to kill its leader. However, in a context where shrines of Asclepius and his father, Apollo, were revered, Jesus established himself as a healer. He cast out demons, restored the leper, healed a woman with a flow of blood, and healed the deaf and the blind. In public displays of power and upon being requested, he healed people from a distance. In the previous chapter, we have seen how healers such as Asclepius, Apollo, or Demeter were celebrated through festivals, dance, and songs. Located close to nearby shrines of Asclepius and Apollo found

---

65. Douglas, *Purity and Danger*, 63.

Jesus, the Best Capernaum Folk-Healer

at Hammath, Emmaus,[66] the Sea of Galilee, Neapolis, Ascalon, Bethsaida, Magdala, and Bethsaida, it is plausible to say the Jesus household in Capernaum knew about their rival healer. How did they celebrate their newly established healer? Using perspectives of form, redaction, narrative, orality, performance, and festival criticism explained in chapter 1, the next chapter reconstructs how the healing stories were performances in celebration of Jesus as the best folk healer.

66. Several places were called Emmaus in Palestine and Mark seems to suggest existence of another Emmaus in Galilee close to Capernaum.

Chapter 5

Mark and Aretalogy concerning the Best Folk Healer—Jesus

INTRODUCTION

USING THEORETICAL PERSPECTIVES OF form, reduction, orality, performance, and festival criticism, explained in chapter 1, this chapter interprets the healing stories in Mark's gospel as celebratory performances within the household performed in celebration of Jesus as the best folk healer. The indirect and direct analogues concerning praise-giving from the Dondo people of southeastern Zimbabwe and those from Greco-Roman context, respectively, adds social scientific interpretation regarding the form and context of the stories. With the background knowledge of Asclepius and Apollo overlapping with Jewish and Christian religion at villages of Hammath, Emmaus, the Sea of Galilee, Neapolis, Ascalon, Bethsaida, Magdala, and Bethsaida, how were the healing stories told? In looking at the healing stories in Mark as celebration narrations concerning Jesus as healer, we look into (i) description of the sickness, focusing on the nature of the condition; (ii) various possible healing methods and other healers; and (iii) the presentation of Jesus as healer. In narrating each of these complex sicknesses, plausibly, Mark puts his audience to their feet in celebrating their healer. In addition to praising Jesus as the best folk healer in Capernaum, I argue that the stories have an identity-formation implication of making the followers aware that, in Jesus, they have the best folk healer whose fame and power is unmatched by rival healers.

MARK'S PRESENTATION OF JESUS

Mark wants his listeners to understand that Jesus is bringing something new.[1] The story is divided into two sections (1:1—8:26; 8:27—16:8), and half of the first section (1:1—3:12) deals with the main character Jesus and his disciples. Within the narrative, the disciples revealed Jesus' identity and, sometimes their posture of doubt resonated with the audience. Jesus is the healer and teacher sent by God—he heals, casts out demons, and forgives sins, making him attract the suspicion and hatred of the religious leaders. I concur with Eugene Boring that, in Mark, Jesus founds a community within which God's power is demonstrated through healing, love, and commensality.[2] Mark 1:1—3:6 portrays Jesus as a healer who is on the move throughout Capernaum and performing major successes in healing.[3] At the onset, Mark wants the listeners to understand that Jesus is "divine" and his power supersedes any force of power. Powerful demons succumbed to his power while contagious diseases vanished by his pronouncement. However, unique to Jesus' manner of healing was his power and effective healing seen in the instant healing that he performed. By doing so, Mark seems to indirectly make his listeners compare Jesus to Asclepius's thermal baths in Tiberius and Gadara. Unlike healers who incubate or follow prolonged rituals, Jesus' unique healing rituals are his instant touch or command, which makes him a better healer than those found in the region; he is the best folk healer. I agree with Hector Avalos, who says that the rise of Christianity, with its renewal of monolatry, instant healing through faith, instant healing from afar, and not charging fees, made Christianity an attractive healing movement that attracted followers, mostly those who were left out by the exclusive Jewish health-care system.[4]

INTRODUCING THE HEALER (MARK 1:1–2)

Unlike Matthew and Luke, Mark starts with healing stories rather than birth myths which ties his Christology closely to Jesus' healing capacity. From the onset, Mark wants the audience to understand Jesus as the healer with power derived from God. In commenting on Mark's presentation of the

1. Guelich, *Mark 1—8:28*, 47.
2. Boring, *Mark*, 57.
3. Beavis, *Mark*, 46.
4. Avalos, *Health Care*, 81.

Mark and Aretalogy concerning the Best Folk Healer—Jesus

healing stories, Laurence McGinley suggests that the healing stories "depict the multitude responding after the manner of a chorus." He further adds, "Choral ending is also characteristic of another group of gospel stories."[5] His suggestion agrees with the analogue illustrated in chapters 2 and 3. To engage in such reading or reconstruction, we need to imagine the odes or atmosphere at any of Asclepius's shrines in Tiberius or near Capernaum that were characterized by lively music and ululations.

Similar to praise-giving, Mark begins by detailing the ancestry of the healer—Jesus. If anything in this section, we are interested in how Mark praises Jesus' ancestry. Unlike Matthew and Luke, who have elaborate genealogies of Jesus, Mark has a different way of introducing Jesus to his household. Mark begins his aretalogy toward Jesus with a statement that indicates Jesus' origin and source of power, saying, Ἀρχὴ τοῦ εὐαγγελίου Ἰησοῦ Χριστοῦ Υἱοῦ Θεοῦ (the beginning of the gospel of Jesus Christ the Son of God). This opening statement can be understood from the cultural conception of power. As we saw in chapters 2 and 3, genealogies served the purpose of revealing derived power and honor. Within Greco-Roman society, power was a commodity associated with one's honor, it was the ability to influence and exert authority over others. With power, one can engage in warfare and win. Mostly such men had resources in terms of slaves and clients who would report to them. Power was intertwined with one's honor and it was hierarchical and yet contested. If one loses power or ability to dominate, equally, his honor is lost. Household leaders, kings, magistrates, governors, and emperors had acquired power and honor based on the influence they had over others. In contrast, slaves had no honor, since their bodies were owned by their captors. In addition, one can have derived power within a patron-client setup. Within such a setting, the powerful person protects the less powerful in exchange of patronage. For example, Herod the Great and his son Herod Antipas of Galilee had derived power from the Romans. In exchange, they ruled on behalf of the Romans. Equally the question by Pilate and the Sanhedrin to Jesus regarding where he derived his power (Mark 11:28) was meant to determine the source of authority behind Jesus' activity.

Given this context, the genealogies serve the purpose of tracing lineage and inherited honor or power. As we noticed in chapter 4, in most Panhellenic victory odes, it was customary to start by revealing the genealogy and place of birth of a hero. We noticed in the previous chapters

---

5. McGinley, "Form-Criticism," 451.

that narrating the genealogy of a hero had the purpose of revisiting the past fame or honor and framing the current victory within the context of previous honor. Mary Ann Beavis comments that in Greek literature, introductions (*prooimia*) were essential for introducing the main character and arousing the interest of the audience.⁶ In the previous chapters, we found similar paeans concerning genealogy of gods such as Apollo, Asclepius, Demeter, and Hermes.

Importantly and similar to victory odes, Mark connects Jesus' genealogy to God—Ἀρχὴ τοῦ εὐαγγελίου Ἰησοῦ Χριστοῦ Υἱοῦ Θεοῦ (The beginning of the gospel of Jesus Christ, the Son of God). In doing so, Mark wants his audience to imagine Jesus as a hero who comes from the strongest genealogy. We saw from the perspective of Zimbabwe's Ndau people or Greco-Roman odes that recitation of the person's origin or genealogy is accompanied by ululation. It is plausible to imagine that the audience to such introduction stood and ululated while others were jumping and praising Jesus. Mentioning the hero to the audience was a highly anticipated occasion of identity impartation. Similar to Greco-Roman odes, the listeners felt that they, too, shared in the identity and accomplishments associated with their hero. To the Greco-Romans, celebrations at a grander scale were done at a public space because they were associated with the identity of the whole community and its gods. Concerning Jesus, we are aware that early Christianity was a small gathering mostly perceived as a schismatic Jewish group. However, though small, Mark wants the occasion to embrace even those who had not yet believed in Jesus as Messiah and best healer. Standing in front of his community, he announced to them, "The beginning of the gospel of Jesus Christ." As we noted in chapter 4, the famous thermal baths of Asclepius at Tiberius, Bethsaida, and Gadara posed the greatest competition to Jesus. Asclepius, the son of Apollo and the Great Zeus was an undisputed god and hero. Indeed, this was a mammoth task for Mark to compete. However, for Mark, he is introducing the Messiah, who is the son of God. Let us see how Mark overturned the fame of such great healers and heroes such as Asclepius toward Jesus.

Mentioning that Jesus is *messiah* and *son of God* is the highest accolade any human can receive. The two titles speak toward Jesus' divinity and mission. Connected to the Jewish background of Joshua, *messiah* was a title associated with a deliverer. To the Jews, a messiah was both a political and priestly figure associated with the new epoch in Yahweh's history with

---

6. Beavis, *Mark*, 30.

his people. The second title, son of God, though common to all people who were regarded as divine, was a political title, since the emperor regarded himself as the supreme son of God.

To Mark's household audience, announcing Jesus' name, the founder of their community, would be a scene associated with great excitement, possibly ululation. Eugene Boring adds that Mark deliberately starts by this statement because of its political resonance.[7] Within the Roman context, the term gospel was associated with military conquest by Augustus, which consequently results in peace and prosperity. Evidence of such semantics is found in the famous Priene of 9 BCE, where Augustus Claudius's victory was described as gospel and peace to the empire.[8] By using similar terminology, Mark equates Jesus' arrival as indication of gospel—good news.

The praise-giving concerning Jesus' origin has effect toward the identity of Mark's household. Plausibly, Mark is fully aware that, by far, the emperor and Asclepius have greater fame than Jesus. To answer this question we need to remind ourselves of the intersection of class and status in the worship of gods. In chapter 3, we noted that gods such as Hermes and Serapis were worshipped by the plebeian class at Delphi.[9] These saw their own experiences of being outsiders and poor resonating with the character of such gods. Similarly, Mark is engaging in identity contestation by undermining the glory of the emperor and, implicitly, that of Asclepius by glorifying Jesus. Arguably while the emperor is welcomed at the grand stadiums of Antioch and Sepphoris and Asclepius at Pergamum and Tiberius, Jesus is welcomed into the household. In doing so, Jesus is the god of the villages, of the outcast, the poor, and sick, with whom he forms an alternative household. The orator is keen in making the distinction that Jesus' beginning (Ἀρχὴ) comes from God and is indicative of the new dispensation of healing and peace. Why is Jesus' divinity important to the orator? The answer could be that Mark is aware that emperors derived their power from genealogy and victories.

With such background in the minds of the listeners, seemingly, Mark argues that Jesus should be given the loudest ululation because his power is derived from God. By using the genitive Υἱοῦ Θεοῦ Mark is downplaying imperial discourse. Instead, Mark is contesting such superiority by suggesting that Jesus derives succession from God and not from the Olympian

---

7. Boring, *Mark*.
8. Evans, "Mark's Incipit," 15.
9. Clay, *Politics of Olympus*, 2.

gods such as Zeus and Cronos. Intentionally, Mark wants the listeners to ask that: if proclamation that is supposed to be proclaimed in Tiberius and Sepphoris are now announced within the household, does it mean that, metaphorically, the empire has been replaced by the household?

I agree with Eric Stewart, who in his book *Gathered around Jesus*, and by use of narrative and space theory, argues that Mark presents Jesus as an alternative geographic center to Jerusalem and Rome.[10] Poignantly, Eric Stewart remarks that throughout Mark's gospel, Jesus receives the sick, many people come to him, he sends disciples away, and the religious leaders also come to him.[11] Jesus brings order, rather than the Romans. In using and labeling Jesus as "the son of God," a title that suggests divinity, Mark is creating alternative and contesting space of divinity around Jesus opposite to that given to the emperor, Apollo and Asclepius.

From this, the Markan community should know that they are not receiving the mere "son of Mary" into the household, instead they are receiving "a god." Coming from the perspective of Luke's gospel, Halvor Moxnes adds that Jesus is instituting an alternative household, an economic institution based on commensality.[12] To the orator, the listeners must understand that true and genuine power resides within the household, the new kingdom, and not the empire. The household is where true power resides and by comparing the household to the empire, Mark is deconstructing and contesting the glory of Rome. True and genuine gospel is in the household with Jesus, whose genealogy is from God.

If we picture Mark's introduction of Jesus in the dusty village of Capernaum, we then start to realize that the narrative has identity implications. To the audience and concerning their identity, hearing that Jesus is the Messiah and son of God would be great news, received with great ululation and possibly dancing. We saw in Pindar's victory praises of heroes such as Hieron of Sicily that a hero lifts up the glory of a city. In a village where no famous god or hero has ever come, now they have their own Messiah and son of a God. In comparison to nearby cities such as Sepphoris and Tiberius, Capernaum was not even close in terms of fame and reputation. In doing so, Mark is essentializing the importance of this occasion by reminding the villagers that, they too, are welcoming a hero whose attributes are the same as that of the emperor and far better than that of Asclepius. Concerning

10. Stewart, "Gathered around Jesus," 224.
11. Stewart, "Gathered around Jesus," 224.
12. Moxnes, *Putting Jesus in His Place*, 154.

Mark and Aretalogy concerning the Best Folk Healer—Jesus

the venue and from reference to a "home" in Mark 3:19, Elizabeth Malbon thinks that Jesus may have his own house in Capernaum which was used as a meeting venue.[13] At some point, after following John the Baptist for a while, Jesus moved to Capernaum, where he established his movement and his own house. Using insights from public celebrations performed to the heroes and gods, we can imagine that the occasion was accompanied with dance and ululations. The fishermen who are represented by the Zebedee brothers and the peasant villagers could be imagined as dancing on the dusty streets of Capernaum.

After connecting Jesus to God, Mark draws John the Baptist into Jesus' ministry lineage. Why? In Luke's gospel, John is Jesus' cousin. However, Mark is interested in what John represents. Like Jesus, John the Baptist called out a community of outcasts—preaching repentance and baptizing people. In addition under Herod, John's death brought memories of similar persecutions by family members and Roman officials toward the household (Mark 13). As we have seen with the plebeian's worship of Hermes and Serapis, the god's identity becomes a collective community social identity. Besides giving memories of persecution, the memory of John is connected with ideas of a keeper or shepherd; that God sends a messenger in the form of John to guard Israel—the community (Exod 23:20). Unlike the one given to Gentiles for proselytizing them, John baptized people toward the arrival of the Messiah and the establishment of the alternative household.[14] Vis-à-vis the temple and Rome, whose values were based on exclusion, the household shall be a space of acceptance and hospitality.[15] Mark further amplifies Jesus' arrival by arguing that, though senior in age, John is the messenger who prepares the arrival of the true leader of the community—one who like Elijah gives double spirit.

Eugene Boring indicates that, by moving the scene to the wilderness and giving it a cosmic dimension, the narrator joins Jesus to God, thus confirming Jesus' power.[16] We already saw with victory ode singers such as Bacchylides and Pindar that myth-making is central in presenting the extraordinary nature of an event. Thus, Jesus is introduced using mythical language—God's voice, wilderness, Satan, and angels—thus signifying

---

13. Malbon, "OIKIA AUTOU," 283.
14. Beavis, *Mark*, 34.
15. Boring, *Mark*, 40.
16. Boring, *Mark*, 33.

the extraordinary nature of Jesus' character.[17] The task of the messenger is preparing the way ὁδός, of the Lord, which symbolically refers to the way from Galilee to the cross. However, I have a different construction of the ὁδός. Building upon Moxnes's comments that the listeners of the way are those within the household, the ὁδός could also mean creating a way for those in the agora, outcasts and those at the banks of the river to travel to their new household. The "way of the Lord" is of those who reject the patriarchal household to join the new household. The theme of the wilderness is a crucial hermeneutical theme predicated on moral regeneration and new beginning. Since the wilderness in the Old Testament signifies new beginning, Mark wants the hearers to known that Jesus is inaugurating a new community based on reliance upon God.[18]

CELEBRATING THE HEALER'S VICTORY OVER DEMONS (MARK 1:27-28)

Announcing the Adversary (Demon in the Synagogue)

Healing and exorcism stories are very much similar to the victory odes in that they, too, narrate the great deeds of a god or hero. We noticed that in the victory odes, the praise singer would highlight the strength of a hero and how the hero gained his victory through highlighting the strength of the horses used in the horse chariot race. Equally, in wrestling matches the focus would be on the bodily physic, the strength shown through various bodily limbs. In patriarchal cultures that celebrate masculinity, power, honor, and fame are intertwined social variables. In commenting on each, it is important to notice the presentation of power of the healer (Jesus), the condition of the sick person and then the process of healing. All this is meant to heighten praise toward the healer. Like Apollo, a great healer is known for the number of victories that are recounted to his honor.

Discursively and for the purpose of Mark's narrative, why did Mark begin with relating the casting out of demons in the synagogue? Arguably, demon possession has similar aspects of power contestation. In addition, we need to understand the cultural phenomenology of demonology. Within

---

17. Malbon, "OIKIA AUTOU," 283.
18. Boring, *Mark*, 39.

the Talmud, various views exist regarding the meaning of demonology and mental illness. According to Hector Avalos and John Pilch, most Jewish folk and those within the popular healing sectors believed that demons are spirits that enter a person and change his or her behavior, and there was no known therapy to demon possession. Hence, since they change a person's original state, mental illness and conditions similar to epilepsy were regarded as caused by demons. Equally, deviant behavior such as prostitution, violence, and all actions that seem not to conform to culturally expected behavior were regarded as caused by demons. The Greek term *moria* was used to refer to persons whose ethical behavior (adultery, stealing, etc.) was culturally unacceptable. A similar term was used for a man who acts out of stupidity. In the Mishnah an example is given of a man who took his precious belongs, silver and gold, and threw them into the sea and destroyed his house. Such behaviors of stupidity were defined as conduct caused by demon possession. Jewish rabbis even define weird behavior such as walking alone at night or taking a walk at grave sites during the night as behavior associated with being possessed by a demon. Darkness and places such as grave sites were believed to be abodes for demons. At the grave sites, demons can tamper with the corpses and vandalize the tombs. Concerning this, Jude 1:9 reports concerning the disagreement and fights over Moses' body between the angel Michael and the devil, suggesting that demons could take dead bodies. The underlying motif is that demons take over control of the person for their evil intention, rendering the person unable to control oneself or fully functioning. Because of broad definitions of the condition of demonology, different Greek terms were used. For example, *kordiakos* refers to one who is intoxicated and therefore cannot talk unintelligibly or forgets everything. A similar term was used for persons with a condition of Down syndrome. In addition, the terms *shoteh*, meaning a person who lives a vagrant lifestyle or absentmindedness, is indicative of demon possession.[19]

No clear procedure or known medicine existed to cure mental illness, hence Jesus' exorcism of demons would make him famous beyond Palestine. Within the Talmud, various regulations were given regarding persons with signs of demon possession. For example, such persons were not supposed to marry. Complications come when a person showed signs of demon possession after being married. In such cases, because only the man can divorce, the Talmud instructs that the wife should remain married to

---

19. Preuss, *Biblical and Talmudic Medicine*, 14.

the demon-possessed husband. Furthermore, such persons could not testify in court because a possessed person has double personality that could mislead him/her into going against the torah. Various prescriptions were given, and among them is fumigating the house of a demon-possessed person with fish or animal liver. Because of the challenge and lack of procedure to cast out demons, Mark set the stage for what seems like a big celebration.

During the first century, Hippocratic healers such as Soranus of Ephesus, advised various Methodist procedures for people suffering from mental disorder. The Methodists were a branch or group of Greek healers that focused on practical steps to rehabilitate the sick patient toward recovery. Concerning mentally unstable people, Soranus suggested that humane ways of treating the mad person were required. He instructed, "Exercise of the mind through reading, games and even attendance to plays—comedy is good for the pressed, tragedy for the merely foolish."[20] Despite being at a public place such as the synagogue, no indication that the demon-possessed man was there due to instruction related to his condition; leaving us with the hypothesis that Mark wants the story to be understood in the context of divine power confrontation.

Excursus: Demonology and Imperial Presence

Influenced by research from studies on empire and postcolonialism, a majority of New Testament scholars have been persuaded to believe that demon possession is a psychosocial response to imperial oppression. In addition to empire studies and postcolonialism, application of psychological theories inspired by Frantz Fanon resulted in an interpretation that sees demon possession as oblique response to political oppression. From this perspective, the question is what abnormal activities imperial possession induced. The perspective further uses insights from archaeology to argue that politically, the region was under the control of Herod Antipas, who reported to Tiberius Pilate, the governor. As a crossroad junction connecting the east to the west, Capernaum was under the jurisdiction of the centurion who was responsible for peace within the region. They further argue that Tiberius and Sepphoris recently built in the region were visible architectural markers of imperial presence in the region. How did Rome "possess" the region? Scholars such as Jean Frayne, Dominic Crossan, and Richard Horsley

---

20. Nutton, *Ancient Medicine*, 205.

paint a picture of heavy taxation and tribute extracted from the region.[21] For them, the region was demanded to pay 200 talents in form of grain such as wheat and agricultural products such as olives. In addition, one-fourth of the revenue was supposed to be paid after every two years. They conclude that the payment of revenue was a severe blow to the peasants' livelihood. For them, the text of Mark 7, where Jesus accused the Pharisees and Sadducee from Jerusalem of violating the Sabbath and purity rules, is crucial. In the text, Jesus turned the accusation toward the religious leaders by accusing them of disobeying the first mosaic commandment, which was to honor one's father and mother by taking that which was supposed to feed family and giving it to the extractive temple and Rome. Within peasant and subsistence communities, there were no nursing homes or retirement centers that could care for the old. Instead, being old and unable to care for themselves, each household had the duty to look after and provide for their elderly.[22] In my view, while the use of postcolonial and psychological theories adds to the meaning of the story, in this case, the meaning is lost by failure to pay attention to the Jewish health-care system and its emic understanding regarding etiology of mental illness.

Point of Confrontation

I take an emic approach inspired by the views of Hector Avalos and other medical anthropologists who regard demon possession as indicative of a personalistic worldview and, thus, a sociocultural description regarding the etiology of mental illness. From an emic perspective, the villagers in Capernaum did not see demonology as some form of psychological diversion caused by the empire. Instead, demonology was their language of describing conditions such as the ones we see in Mark 1:22–28. Within Jewish cosmology, demon possession meant the individual opened himself to the control of evil spirit that disturbed his mind. Hector Avalos indicates that the Jewish health-care system believed that each illness or pain in any part of the body was triggered by a demon. In view of the prevalence of the

---

21. Freyne, "Herodian Economics"; Crossan, *Historical Jesus*; Horsley and Silberman, *Message and the Kingdom*; Horsley, *Galilee*.

22. Fanon, "Wretched of the Earth." Writing from the perspective of Algerian revolution, Fanon argues that, from fear of confronting the oppressive imperial French regime, the natives resorted to religious frenzy and possession, diverting the reality of oppression to inner demonic possession that needs exorcism.

Jesus, the Best Capernaum Folk-Healer

condition, it seems the demon associated with mental illness was one of the stubborn demons that refuses exorcism, and ability to cast them away implies that the exorcist is powerful (Mark 3:21).[23]

In Mark 1, the casting out of the demon is given within the mythical context of power and territoriality. In Mark 1:23–27, the demon's power is revealed. In expressing power the demon defended itself, saying, *What have we to do with thee, thou Jesus of Nazareth? Art thou come to destroy us? I know thee who thou art, the Holy One of God. And Jesus rebuked him, saying, Hold thy peace, and come out of him. And the unclean spirit, tearing him and crying with a loud voice, came out of him.*

Here, the narrator reveals the demon's power, thereby increasing the victory celebrations toward Jesus. Clearly, as expression of defiance, the demon cried out and protested against Jesus' presence. This indicates the demon's territorial jurisdiction over Capernaum, the synagogue, and surrounding areas. The power of the demon and its taunting toward Jesus is juxtaposed against Jesus' power (ἐξουσίαν) expressed in Mark 1:22. The term power (*exousia*) is found nine times and in all references it is associated with Jesus—the power that he will transfer to his disciples (3:15; 6:7). This continues the theme that Jesus derives power from God and then passes the same authority to the disciples. Such power is distinct from that of the rabbis, which was mediated through the torah and was qualified through votes by religious leaders.[24] Ordinarily upon entering the synagogue, the visitor would be invited to preach, but Jesus is presented as one with agency—he goes into the synagogue to teach. For Mark, teaching, healing, and exorcism are inclusive activities that express the presence of the kingdom of God. Noticeably, the teaching and exorcism is happening in their synagogue which was a public meeting place. Thus, by casting out a demon that was in the synagogue, Jesus is publicly expressing power over a spiritual force which the villagers dreaded. The praise-giving being expressed in Mark 1:22 is attribution of power to Jesus. For Mark's household, the power of Jesus far exceeds that of the synagogue leaders and Rome.

In many Greco-Roman choral or poetic aretalogies, it is the point of victory that is most important. At the point of victory, the audience would celebrate and contrast the power of their god vis-à-vis other gods. We can imagine that the same was happening here when the demon was being defeated. The demons confessed, saying, "Art thou come to destroy us? I know

---

23. Avalos, *Health Care*, 63.
24. Boring, *Mark*, 63.

thee who thou art, the Holy One of God" (1:23). Eugene Boring comments, "Jesus commands the demon to be silent, preventing it from using its knowledge as an apotropaic force"[25] On the other hand, William Lane suggests that the confession is a declaration of recognition of power which should be understood as "you have come to destroy us."[26] Inspired by Pindar's victory songs, I take a slightly different conclusion that the statement by the demon is a strategy of negotiating a less embarrassing defeat. Negotiating for survival is a theme that is prevalent in Pindar's victory songs whereby, facing defeat, the loser negotiates shared victory for his own honor. It was common that, fearing shame from onlookers and community, in a combat, a loser would negotiate for a shared victory. Taking this perspective, the statement by the demon could be read as a direct aretalogy from the enemy's lips; praising Jesus as more powerful, yet negotiating its presence in the synagogue and in the region. If Jesus falls into the trap he would coexist with the demon. In Mark 3:21, upon being accused of working alongside the prince of demons, Beelzebub, Jesus categorically states that he would not share power with the demon. Instead, his mission is to dismantle the demonic strongholds. The kingdom of God introduced at the opening of Mark's story is *euangelion* of power and victory over demons. The negotiation by the demon opens for the next important stage—the casting way of the demon from both the victim and from the synagogue and region.

The Healer's Power and Fame Celebrated

Hector Avalos's remark that Christianity became attractive as an alternative health-care system because of its effective healing rituals and for not charging fee applies here.[27] To the audience, vv. 25–28 are crucial because they were told in the context of loud cheers and celebrations. In these verses Jesus rebukes, silences, and commands the demons to come out. In response, the demon convulsed and cried out. The rebuke ἐπετίμησεν is a clear sign of Jesus' power.[28] Boring explains, "No incantations, no magic, words, no props, no ceremonies or rituals . . . no struggle." A similar reference to rebuke is found in Mark 5 where Jesus casts out the demon in Gadara. Eugene Boring remarks that the fact that there was no struggle or resistance from

25. Boring, *Mark*, 64; Beavis, *Mark*, 53.
26. Lane, *Gospel of Mark*, 74.
27. Avalos, *Health Care*, 80.
28. Stein, *Mark*, 89.

Jesus, the Best Capernaum Folk-Healer

the demon signifies the undisputed power of Jesus.[29] Instead, "Jesus stands before a defeated enemy, an enemy that knows it is defeated."[30] Heightening the power of the victor is important identity formation to the audience. The reaction of convulsion and crying out is important point in heightening the celebration. R. T. France comments that the convulsion and crying out are a sign of the demon's "desperation but ineffectual resistance."[31] Guelich remarks that the crying by the demons is indicative of a death wail.[32] This is the tipping point of the demon's authority and could be regarded as the most celebrated section of the story. I suggest that the performance of convulsion and crying out were exhibited through exaggerated gestures that amused the audience. It is possible to imagine that the performer imitated the condition of convulsion by writhing on the floor. Equally, following the pattern and emotion of a defeated worrier in a battle, the performer may have imitated the crying by the demon through expression of loud sorrowful voice. While doing this, the audience would be celebrating upon realizing that their oppressive enemy has been defeated. A psychological identity formation of shared victory would engulf the listeners. Using coded language of demonology, the defeat of the demon is psychologically transferred as their own victory. Like a Greco-Roman hero who won in battle, Jesus' celebration and victory were shared moments by the Jesus household.

Similar to paean sung to Apollo or Asclepius which ends with glorifying the fame of the hero, Mark ends the exorcism that took place in the synagogue with a remark, saying, "And they were all amazed, so that they questioned among themselves, saying, 'What is this? A new teaching with authority! He commands even the unclean spirits, and they obey him.' And at once his fame spread everywhere throughout all the surrounding region of Galilee" (vv. 27–28). On several sections in the book, Mark refers to Jesus' fame (cf. 1:45; 3:7; 5:20; 6:54–56; 7:36–37).[33] In the previous chapters, we find similar praising about fame toward the gods. For example, in praising Asclepius and his children, Aristides sang, "Asclepius, a god most famous, le Paian!"

From the victory odes, the hero's fame is derived from his victories. Equally, soon after the important victory in the synagogue, Mark starts to

---

29. Boring, *Mark*; Myers, *Binding the Strong Man*; Horsley, *Hearing the Whole Story*.
30. Boring, *Mark*, 65.
31. France, *Gospel of Mark*, 105.
32. Guelich, *Mark 1—8:28*, 58.
33. Beavis, *Mark*, 53.

report regarding Jesus' fame. To healers, fame is connected to many other social aspects such as honor and the amount of followers. Mark recounts, "And the report of him went out straightaway everywhere into all the region of Galilee round about" (Mark 1:28). David Marshal discussed the theme of fame within the prism of media celebrity culture and notes that fame is associated with individuals whom society regard as public ideals.[34] Fame includes actions, personality, and achievements associated with an individual. Psychologists comment that when fame is achieved, the individual or achiever receives cultlike status from the public, which puts pressure on the individual to keep up with the celebrity image. When an individual fails to maintain the celebrity image, it may lead to depression or even suicide. Several types of fame exist—immortality, spiritual, and worldly fame.[35] Concerning Jesus, Mark seems interested in immortality and spiritual fame. Immortality fame could be applied to the manner in which Jesus' deeds and actions were regarded as having universal value. Spiritual fame speaks to how Jesus lived his life in accordance with God's will. Like honor, fame is defined vis-à-vis other forms of fame, Mark's reference to Jesus' fame that had spread to surrounding regions makes us ask about who else's fame existed in the region. Indeed as noted, Asclepius's shrines existed in Tiberius and Sepphoris, while other Jewish healers were found in Capernaum. In view of this, Mark is deliberate by stretching Jesus' fame from Capernaum to the entire region of Galilee. In doing so, fame has identity formation within Mark's household by insisting in telling his community that they are following a healer whose fame is wider. Without explicitly mentioning it, Mark's aretalogy regarding Jesus' fame that had spread within Galilee is intended to make Jesus a renowned healer within the region whose fame surpasses that of other healers.

ARETALOGY OVER THE HEALER WHO CARE FOR THE WEAK (MARK 1:29-32)

In the previous chapter, we have seen that Asclepius's children—Ponderilius, Machaon, and Hygiea—were celebrated for their healing which was indicative of care and benevolence. Healing and welfare were some of the main variables that define a good god which would attract many followers

---

34. Marshall, *Celebrity and Power*, 27.
35. Giles, *Illusions Immortality*, 5.

to the god's shrine. Similarly, the story concerning Jesus' healing of Peter's mother-in-law celebrates Jesus' care over the sick.

The orator quickly concluded the scene in the synagogue and shifted the attention of his audience toward the street and then the house of Peter's mother-in-law. Mary Ann Beavis notices that the story is characterized by quick narrative movement indicated by the word "immediately."[36] It is possible that, while walking to Peter's mother-in-law, those who had witnessed the exorcism and possibly the family of the restored man, walked behind Jesus, celebrating him as the best healer. The story concerning the healing of Peter's mother-in-law also needs to be analyzed in terms of the story expressing (a) the challenge or problem, (b) the presentation of the power of the healer, and then (c) the celebration that the story evokes. As the story opens, we are not told the herbal remedies or other healers that the mother had consulted. Also, no background information regarding how Peter initiated the story about the sickness of his mother-in-law. However, from the first story regarding the exorcism in the synagogue, it is plausible that, upon witnessing the powerful healing in the synagogue, Peter requested Jesus to come and heal his mother-in-law. However, though no mention of medical remedies taken before Jesus came, we are given the hint that she had been sick for a while, making her unable to fulfill her domestic duties. Given this background, we can assume that she had taken some known herbs regarding her sickness.[37] In terms of hierarchy of healing and like most cultures, self-help medicine is the first level in seeking healing. At the domestic level, household members usually look for various herbs and diet. If this fails, then a local herbalist or divine healer is consulted. Pharmaceuticals and healers that require money are usually the last resort after exhausting other avenues.[38]

The extent of her condition corresponds to the celebrations that would take place after she is restored. Noticeably, her story is very brief and devoid of much detail. The orator simply remarks, "Now Simon's mother-in-law lay ill with a fever, and immediately they told him about her. And he came and took her by the hand and lifted her up, and the fever left her, and she began to serve them" (Mark 1:30–31). In the past, the story has been regarded as reinforcing the theme of service or *diakonia* to Jesus and

36. Beavis, *Mark*, 53.
37. Avalos, *Health Care*, 3.
38. Avalos, *Health Care*, 91.

that, in Mark, "women are models of faith."[39] Based on her service to Jesus and the disciples, the other dominant reading is approaching the story as a model for hospitality. Some scholars focus on the form of the story, thus reading it as tradition that came from Peter.[40] Observations have also been made concerning the fact that the story is spatially categorized between the synagogue where the exorcism took place and now the house setting. Away from the crowd, in Mark's gospel, the house setting is a private place for instruction.[41]

In most commentaries, remarks concerning the actual healing are brief. For example, William Lane remarks that during ancient times, fever was regarded as a disease and not as a symptom of a bodily condition. On the other hand, Robert Guelich puts focus on the fact that Jesus healed by transferring power from himself to the patient. In antiquity, spiritual healers were regarded as embodying divine power and, by touching them, one can be healed (see Mark 3:10; 8:22; 5:28; 6:56).[42]

Let us reread the story from the perspective of praise-giving, looking at the extent of the problem, the presentation of the healer's attributes, and the confrontation with the sickness. Concerning fever, Vivian Nutton explains that in antiquity fever in the body was believed to be inversion by a demon.[43] However, later Hippocratic writings, especially by Galen, associate fever to change in weather and climate. They note that low-lying marshes and proximity to grassy and wet conditions likely results in the person having a fever. With reference to dense regions of Macedonia and Boeotia, Nutton further comments that malaria had existed in the Mediterranean region since the Neolithic period.[44] Diagnosis includes checking the body temperature by putting a hand on the neck or forehead of the patient. The Talmud prescribes that, if the temperature is too high for more than two days, then bloodletting should be administered. Bloodletting, venesection of phlebotomy, was a common healing practice that comes from the belief that disease resides in the blood. Hence, they believed that bloodletting would assist in reducing the concentration of blood imbalance.[45] In addi-

---

39. Beavis, *Mark*, 53.
40. Guelich, *Mark 1—8:28*, 62; France, *Gospel of Mark*, 107.
41. France, *Gospel of Mark*, 107.
42. Lane, *Gospel of Mark*, 77; Guelich, *Mark 1—8:28*, 62.
43. Nutton, *Ancient Medicine*, 32.
44. Nutton, *Ancient Medicine*, 32.
45. Rosner, *Medicine in the Bible and the Talmud*, 151.

Jesus, the Best Capernaum Folk-Healer

tion, herbal treatment was a common therapy. Since fever was regarded as a disease associated with low-lying areas, arrangements were also made that during summer and wet weather, people moved to upstairs rooms or relocated to regions with a higher altitude. Because of lack of modern treatment, many ancient cities were deserted and populations declined due to deaths.[46]

Taking this context, and though the healing story of Peter's mother-in-law is brief, we are dealing with a huge and potentially fatal situation. Located in Capernaum which was close to the lake of Galilee, it is likely that Peter's mother-in-law may have been suffering from malaria or any other sickness associated with being close to the lake. The story reports that she had been lying for days with fever, perhaps indicating a deteriorating progression concerning her bodily condition. If unattended for the next few days, her liver and entire body would fail, which would lead to her death.

The narrative line of Jesus as best healer develops after the recent healing from the synagogue and possibly, people who witnessed the synagogue healing and those who saw people moving toward the house drew closer, some due to curiosity while others expected a repetition of the synagogue event. The orator says that Jesus went to the place where she was laying and touched her then lifted her up, resulting in the fever leaving her body. The narrative echoes similar healing strategies by healers whose power magically restores the sick upon touching them. Upon witnessing such sudden restoration, the audience would celebrate the power of Jesus who is an instant healer. Unlike Asclepius who incubates the patients over night to receive healing through dreams or other magical experiences, Jesus healed through instant touch. One would imagine that some started to sing and dance in praise of Jesus, the instant healer. In a village area such as Capernaum, news of instant healing of Peter's mother-in-law would travel fast through women when they meet at the wells or men during their gathering at the synagogue, fields, or at the lake while fishing. To those who have visited local healing shrines of Asclepius in Bethsaida, Sepphoris, or in Tiberius, such instant healing would tilt favor toward Jesus and most would repeat the remark said at the synagogue: "What is this? A new teaching with authority! He commands even the unclean spirits, and they obey him."

---

46. Nutton, *Ancient Medicine*, 32.

Mark and Aretalogy concerning the Best Folk Healer—Jesus

PRAISE-GIVING CONCERNING THE HEALING OF MANY PEOPLE (MARK 1:33-34)

The healing of many people during the evening can be understood similarly to praise-giving toward Apollo and Asclepius. Mark narrates, "That evening at sundown they brought to him all who were sick or oppressed by demons. And the whole city was gathered together at the door. And he healed many who were sick with various diseases, and cast out many demons. And he would not permit the demons to speak, because they knew him" (Mark 1:33-34). William Lane makes interesting remarks that the two verses are summary comments connected to the previous healing. In addition, seen from repetition of "many" and "all" the orator wants the listeners to acknowledge that the crowd flocked to Jesus for healing.[47] Being a Sabbath, perhaps the people delayed until evening to bring their sick relatives. Given that the healing took place within the house, Mark is generalizing the presence of crowd, however, we should excuse him of his excitement of the arrival of Jesus in Capernaum.[48] In terms of narrative progression, the healing of the crowd during the evening gives spatial movement from the synagogue to the house and now back to the public space and also setting the context for the opposition with the religious leaders (see Mark 2:23-28; 3:1-6).[49]

Using insights from praise-giving, the healing at night serves two functions—first, that of shifting the narrative space from the house where healing of an individual took place to the public place where attention is now toward the crowd. Second, here we see the combination of the growing fame and that of celebration blended together. As the crowd gathered to receive healing, they celebrated and took the fame to their communities. In the previous chapter, we have seen similar praise toward the sons of Asclepius—Machaon and Podalirius—whose fame exceeds that of the Egyptian healers and Hippocrates.[50] In a similar fashion, Mark remarks, "And he healed many who were sick with various diseases, and cast out many demons. And he would not permit the demons to speak, because they knew him." I concur with Robert Guelich that phrases such as "many people" and "many demons" indicates a pre-Markan tradition developed

---

47. Lane, *Gospel of Mark*, 79.
48. France, *Gospel of Mark*, 110.
49. Guelich, *Mark 1—8:28*, 54.
50. Russell et al., *In Praise of Asclepius*, 35.

Jesus, the Best Capernaum Folk-Healer

from the context of praise-giving. Instead of seeing the statement as use of hyperbolic language or a general remark, it is plausible to read it as aretological narrative of praise-giving whose aim is to celebrate the healer whose skills are far better than those in the region. Equally, that Jesus did "not permit the demons to speak, because they knew him" belongs to the motif of Jesus casting out demons after silencing them.[51] Using praise-giving as a lens, it is plausible to argue that reference toward "many" people who were healed and the silencing of demons is akin to praise-giving found in the victory odes. The silencing of demons indicates that Jesus has power over all forms of sickness. In recreating the scene and mood, such statements evoke cheers and ululations by the audience as they celebrate their local healer whose fame and power exceeds that of Asclepius, whose shrines were located in Tiberius, Bethsaida, and Sepphoris.

PRAISE-GIVING OVER THE HEALING OF A MAN WITH LEPROSY (MARK 1:40–45)

In looking into the praise-giving over the healing of the man with leprosy, we need to understand the experience of having leprosy, the presentation of Jesus as healer, and the possible celebration associated with the telling of such a story. Leprosy was a common skin disease during the Greco-Roman period, among the Jews and many other cultures. It was regarded as evidence of punishment from the gods. In the Old Testament the disease was associated with Ba'al Zevuw, god of the flies, and Josephus mentions the Kyrene people who worship the god who chases away the flies.[52] Ferngren cautions us that in ancient times, due to lack of diagnostic equipment that differentiates particular disease from the others, certain skins conditions ended up being described by similar terms or that similar condition received different terminology.[53] This is true with leprosy. For example, the term *sherim* is used in reference to conditions such as "skin lesions, scabs, boils, scars, eczema, burn wounds," while *zara'at* is used in reference to conditions such as "leprosy, elephantiasis, syphilis, diphtheria, viola or some other malady."[54] Furthermore, no specific cause was given for the various skin conditions. Religious groups thought that the disease was due

51. Guelich, *Mark 1—8:28*, 66.
52. Rosner, *Medicine in the Bible and the Talmud*, 75.
53. Ferngren, *Medicine and Health Care*, 16.
54. Baden and Moss, "Origin and Interpretation of Ṣāraʿat," 643.

to curse by the gods. Equally, myths exist that the skin disease was caused by the flies or insects that stay in the brain of the patient. Given that flies constantly follow the patient due to smell, this may plausibly explain why insects and flies were connected to the disease.[55] Connected to this, the term *ra'atan* was also used to refer to skin disease. People with skin disease associated with sexually transmitted disease, syphilis, were believed to give birth to children with bodily defects and in some cases, they were impotent. For example, it is believed that the Egyptian pharaoh who took Sarah from Abraham as wife was suffering from a certain sexual condition that resulted in him not to have children. Blood from both the male or female's genital organs were believed to be due to *ra'atan*. Citing the Ketubot 77b, Rosner says, "If a man had intercourse immediately after being bled, he will have feeble or nervous or cachectic children. If intercourse took place after both the man and woman were bled, they will have children afflicted with ra'atan. Rabbi Papa said: this is only so in the case where nothing was eaten (after the bleeding)."[56]

The cure for *ra'atan* involves taking a complex mixture of "polion (or penny royal, a fragrant plant), ladanum (a dark brown resinous exudate from the rock rose), rinds of a nut tree, shavings of a dressed hide, melilot (sweet scented clover), and the calyx of a red date tree. These must be boiled together and carried into a house of marble (to shut out all draughts)."[57] After making the mixture, "three hundred cups of the mixture must then be poured on the head of the sufferer from *ra'atan* until his cranium is soft and then his brain is cut open. Then four myrtle leaves are brought and each foot of the insect is then lifted up, and one leaf is placed beneath it this preventing the insect from burying its feet in the brain when lifted out. The insect is then grasped with a pair of tweezers and burned, for otherwise it would return to the patient (ketubot 77b)."[58] Rosner suggests that the process being described is folk medicine used in the treatment of tumor whose "outgrowths resembles the feet of a reptile and whose removal must be accompanied with extreme caution."[59] The Babylonians have other healing procedures that include eating mangold (or beet or tomatoes) and

---

55. Baden and Moss, "Origin and Interpretation of Ṣāraʿat," 643.
56. Rosner, *Medicine in the Bible and the Talmud*, 74.
57. Rosner, *Medicine in the Bible and the Talmud*, 74.
58. Rosner, *Medicine in the Bible and the Talmud*, 75.
59. Rosner, *Medicine in the Bible and the Talmud*, 75.

Jesus, the Best Capernaum Folk-Healer

drink beer made from *cuscuta* of the *hizmi* shrub or "bathe in the waters of the Euphrates."

Commentators to the pericope regarding the man with leprosy observe that the story lacks specific geographic location, which may indicate that Mark found it somewhere and redacted it into his larger literary narrative.[60] As it stands, the story picks up from the theme of Jesus' fame having spread throughout Galilee. Structurally the story seems to suggest double healing—one through ritual cleansing (1:41–43) and the other through rebuke or silencing (1:43) of the demon behind the skin condition.

From the description regarding the disease, leprosy was a dangerous condition. As we noted, the Jewish health-care system regarded people with leprosy as subjects that should be confined outside the city or village boundaries. Commenting on a passage in Luke 17:11–12 concerning a large group of lepers outside the city, Hector Avalos remarks that people with conditions deemed infectious were many and these, possibly, found an alternative healing system in Christianity.[61] Having been labeled as nonfunctional and unwholesome, the man with leprosy suffered ostracization due to his condition. Acquiring leprosy meant losing all social interaction including family. A person with leprosy was akin to a dead person and was cast away from society with no recourse to amend the condition. Consequently, it meant shame to oneself and to the family and village.

Upon asking for and receiving the confession from the man with leprosy, Jesus' reaction was that of anger, which has been interpreted in three ways. Either (i) Jesus was angry toward the religious leaders for their insistence toward the ceremonial law instead of the welfare of the sick; (ii) Jesus was angry at the man with leprosy for reporting and announcing the healing throughout the village; or (iii) Jesus was angry at the leprosy and its curse.[62] Boring's suggestion that Jesus' anger should be read alongside his compassion is the most plausible interpretation. Boring remarks, "Mark tends to categorize everything that threatens the fulfillment of life intended by God, whether sickness or natural evil such as storms as part of the demonic kingdom, so that the cleansing of the leper has overtones of Jesus' confrontation with demonic evil."[63] Arguably, the presentation of Jesus as healer in this story is similar to the one seen in the victory odes toward

---

60. Beavis, *Mark*, 54; Guelich, *Mark 1—8:28*, 73.
61. Avalos, *Health Care*, 68.
62. Stein, *Mark*, 106.
63. Boring, *Mark*, 71.

Mark and Aretalogy concerning the Best Folk Healer—Jesus

Asclepius, who is regarded as a healer with mercy and compassion toward the sick and even toward the animals that had received cruel treatment from their owners. Equally, in the previous chapter, the compassion of Apollo as healer who cares for the well-being of his people is expressed in the Homeric odes. One of the songs concerning Apollo's compassion says, "Hymn the ambrosial gifts that the gods enjoy, and the sorrows which men under the hands of the deathless gods ever suffer, living without understanding and helpless, nor are they ever able to find any cure for their death or defense against old age" (lines 190–94).

As praise-giving, the healing of the man with leprosy excites the crowd or the listeners. Instead of the healing procedures that include herbs and drinks, Jesus uses touch and words. Hector Avalos remarks that Jesus used faith instead of elaborate rituals which made him the best option for those who sought quicker and effective healing.[64] Upon hearing that Jesus healed a man with leprosy by mere pronouncement and touch, such an act would received cheers and ululations within the early Christian households. To the followers of Jesus, the healing is an expression of compassion and power. The fact that Jesus touched and healed the man with a dreaded skin disease puts his power above that of the religious leaders who had chased the man away. Equally, it puts Jesus' power above that of other folk healers who used herbs and elaborate healing processes. Because of his effectiveness, the celebration would capture Jesus as a far better healer than Asclepius and other healers in the region. Instead of silence, the story ends with celebration which possibly captures the mood in the house. The action of the restored man could be regarded as the aretalogy from the household. Verse 45 records, "But he went out and began to talk freely about it, and to spread the news, so that Jesus could no longer openly enter a town, but was out in desolate places, and people were coming to him from every quarter." Robert Stein remarks, "Those who are healed cannot help but preach the good news and spread the word that Jesus of Nazareth is the Christ, the son of God and that he has inaugurated the Kingdom of God." The preaching by the leper "illustrates the greatness of the Son of God, who cannot be hid."[65] The action by the leper echoes post-Easter early Christian evangelism of preaching, announcing, and proclamation.[66] In similar manner, the actions

---

64. Avalos, *Health Care*, 82.
65. Stein, *Mark*, 109.
66. Boring, *Mark*, 72; Collins and Attridge, *Mark*, 108.

of the leper as missionary and evangelist could be regarded as aretalogy regarding Jesus' healing power and compassion.

PRAISE-GIVING CONCERNING THE HEALING OF THE PARALYTIC MAN (MARK 2:1–5)

The healing of the paralytic man opens chapter 2 of Mark's gospel, and similar to the already covered healing stories, we are curious to know the nature of the disease, the presentation of Jesus as the healer, and the possible praise-giving associated with the story. The story progresses from the story of the healed leper who announced to the village regarding his healing which sets up conflict with the religious leaders. Suggestions have been made that this story could be one of the pre-Markan narratives concerning the conflict between Jesus and the religious leaders, thus introducing one of Mark's major themes that Jesus died due to conflict with the religious leaders.[67]

The focus of the story is the paralytic condition of the man upon whom Jesus demonstrated mercy. Besides paralysis, the Talmud deals with several neurological disorders, some of which are due to injury from falling, which results in a damaged spine. Since the belief was that the condition was due to demons, the general diagnosis was exorcism. In addition, oil rubbed on the spin of the patient was recommended.[68] Mark used the term παραλυτικὸν (2:3) which further reveals that the man was unable to walk. From an honor and shame perspective, the paralyzed man was a burden to his family. His condition suggests he could not marry or contribute to the household economy. We are not told about his age, but the designation that he was a man may suggest that he was of mature age. Being carried and requiring assistance for his mobility meant that he was a shame to his family. However, a different perspective from Anna Rebecca Solevåg is that, given that the man was carried by four men, may suggest that the man was not poor. She further argues that Jesus' command to the man to take up his mat and go, may assume that the man was leader of a household. Furthermore, given that the task of carrying a person with disability was the duty of slaves, "It seems plausible that the four helpers in Mark's story are presented as slaves or perhaps family members, rather than friends."[69]

---

67. Collins and Attridge, *Mark*, 182.
68. Rosner, *Medicine in the Bible and the Talmud*, 31.
69. Solevåg, *Negotiating the Disabled Body*, 37.

In response, Solevåg is making a valid claim in suggesting that the man was not poor. However, I have a different view from her assumption that the man was a household owner or that he owns a house. Within dyadic and subsistence societies, a person is identified as being part of a household and members of the household do not own houses rather they build their own separate hut within the homestead. The idea of owning one's own house is a modern and mostly Western socialization of growing up with family and then at a certain age moving out of the parent's house and owning one's own apartment. Within a dyadic context, a more plausible reconstruction which Solevåg mentions but does not give much attention is that the men that carried the paralytic man are fellow household members, either brothers or male extended family members.

Furthermore and given that such conditions were perceived as being cursed by the gods, neighbors would frown upon the household where the man belonged as being cursed and in need of ritual cleansing. However, the story reveals the dyadic nature of the culture by reporting that some men, possibly the relatives, carried the man to Jesus. From a trauma perspective, living with a condition that he could not reverse, the paralyzed man could be described as traumatized. Trauma arises when a person or community is faced with a challenge that one cannot find a breakthrough, and being boxed by a problem and without solution may lead to suicidal thoughts. Thus, in the paralytic man, we are dealing with a helpless, shameful, and traumatizing condition which drained the man of social relevance and cultural honor.

The presentation of Jesus as healer is revealed in Mark's account:

> And many were gathered together, so that there was no more room, not even at the door. And he was preaching the word to them. And they came, bringing to him a paralytic carried by four men. And when they could not get near him because of the crowd, they removed the roof above him, and when they had made an opening, they let down the bed on which the paralytic lay. And when Jesus saw their faith, he said to the paralytic, "Son, your sins are forgiven." (Mark 2:2–5)

Two themes are recurring here: first, the fame and power of Jesus as healer. The fact that "many" gathered to the extent of crowding the entrance points to Jesus' fame. From the previous healing stories, Jesus accumulated fame from being seen as a powerful and effective divine healer. The house being referred to could be Peter's house or that Jesus had his own house in

Capernaum and he turned the house into a healing shrine. Boring remarks, "The private home has become a public place, reminiscent of the house churches of Mark's own time . . . there was not room at the door . . . Mark pictures the increasing attractiveness and drawing power of Jesus and his message."[70] Similarly, Guelich remarks, "The early church perceived Jesus as one who heals the sick and offers his friendship to the sinners."[71]

The praise-giving associated with the story comes from witnessing the conflict from the scribes and the amazement from the crowd. The scribes challenged Jesus for forgiving sins, which to them, only God can do so. In the Jewish worldview, sickness and sin are intertwined given that sickness was regarded as punishment from God. In response to the man's condition and acting on behalf of God, Jesus forgave sin and commanded the man to rise up and take his mat and go.

Using a cross-cultural and imaginative reading based on the Dondo people and praise-giving associated with Apollo and Asclepius, similar to the healings that we find from Apollo and Asclepius which were characterized by impossibility, Jesus performed an impossible healing. In reaction, the crowd celebrated and shouted, ὅτι Οὕτως οὐδέποτε εἴδαμεν (We never saw anything like this!, v. 12). Such a statement was likely accompanied by celebrations from the family and the onlookers. Jesus is the healer of the impossible conditions. We have seen similar rhetoric given to Asclepius concerning healing various ailments. Similarly, we can imagine that the celebrations by the family and the crowd spilled into the streets as people sang and shouted on their way to their household. The evidence of the once-paralyzed man who is now walking and jumping would add to the atmosphere of celebration. Upon witnessing the restoration, amazement would be accompanied by chants of, "We never saw anything like this! We never saw anything like this! We never saw anything like this!" The chanting would increase as the crowd approached the man's household where his healing would translate to his restored honor and dignity.

PRAISE-GIVING CONCERNING A MAN WITH WITHERED HAND (MARK 3:1–6)

Following Boring's structure, the healing of the man with the withered hand on a Sabbath corresponds with the healing of the paralytic man. Both

---

70. Boring, *Mark*, 76.
71. Guelich, *Mark 1—8:28*, 82.

speak concerning showing kindness vis-à-vis following the Sabbath laws. Thematically and in terms of form, the story builds upon previous stories regarding controversies with the religious leaders—controversy of the healing of the paralyzed man on Sabbath (2:1–12), eating with tax collectors and sinners (2:13–17), controversy over fasting (2:18–22), and controversy over Sabbath (2:23–28).[72] The withering of his hand symbolizes lack of life and the healing is reported similar to resurrection whereby life was restored. Similar to the condition of a paralyzed man, withering of hand had implications toward the man's honor and relevance within the household. With a withered hand, the man had limited duties around the household and religiously, he was regarded as being cursed by the gods.

The presentation of Jesus as the healer is intertwined with the opposition from the religious leaders who, by now, were frustrated by constant breach of religious laws by Jesus and wanted to devise ways of killing him. The religious leaders had jurisdiction over all religious and cultural matters and could pronounce punishment over deviants such as Jesus. However, to give such a severe punishment they needed permission from the Roman officials in the region. Mark says that they too were in attendance on that particular Sabbath and looked with great interest toward Jesus' behavior. This time, no request from the patient regarding his condition, instead, Jesus initiated the healing. He framed the debate around the moral and spiritual intention of the Sabbath, saying, "Is it lawful on the Sabbath to do good or to do harm, to save life or to kill?" (3:4). Boring remarks, "The incident focuses the issue of the purpose of the Torah, namely to bring life and to do God's will, ultimately expressed in the love command by which all commandments are to be judged."[73] In expressing love and mercy, the man is in need of urgent restoration from the condition that had metaphorically "withered" his life from full life. The silence and refusal by the religious leaders to grant life but instead attending to the moral and spiritual side of the torah made Jesus angry. Mark reports, "And he looked around at them with anger, grieved at their hardness of heart" (v. 5). Like the Egyptian Pharaoh, the religious leaders are refusing the will of God of life and love upon the man. Jesus' anger is predicated upon the fact that those who were given the responsibility to provide life and love are, metaphorically, "withering" life by refusing healing.

---

72. Boring, *Mark*; Guelich, *Mark 1—8:28*, 132.

73. Boring, *Mark*, 94.

Jesus, the Best Capernaum Folk-Healer

The praise-giving associated with this story is clear; Jesus is a compassionate healer vis-à-vis the religious leaders. Associated with this could be the celebration that Jesus acted on behalf of God and not the people. We can assume that the family and the restored man celebrated his healing with jubilation. Building up on previous testimonies of healing, the news concerning the restored hand traveled throughout the village. On traveling back his household, celebrations accompanied him in the streets and full celebrations were done upon arriving at the household. The man's capacity to act as a full household member was restored. He can now own and cultivate land and do all the domestic duties associated with being a man. His shame has been removed and he can now walk with the honor associated with full-bodied men.

In the previous chapters, we have seen similar aretalogies concerning mercy attributed to Apollo and Asclepius. Importantly, a merciful god who promptly attends to the concerns of the followers attracted many adherents. Thus, it is no surprise seeing the growing followers and fame of Jesus around the village of Capernaum. Concerning the growing crowd, Mark remarks,

> Jesus withdrew with his disciples to the sea, and a great crowd followed, from Galilee and Judea and Jerusalem and Idumea and from beyond the Jordan and from around Tyre and Sidon. When the great crowd heard all that he was doing, they came to him. And he told his disciples to have a boat ready for him because of the crowd, lest they crush him, for he had healed many, so that all who had diseases pressed around him to touch him. And whenever the unclean spirits saw him, they fell down before him and cried out, "You are the Son of God." And he strictly ordered them not to make him known. (Mark 3:7–12)

It is possible that the above verses came from pre-Markan healing stories that emphasize Jesus' healing power and fame. In the above verses, while the motif concerning silence remains, from here onward, Mark is comfortable in letting the listeners know that the healings pulled the crowd toward Jesus. Mark wants the listeners to understand that all directions and regions around Capernaum heard about the fame of Jesus as the healer and such healing power goes beyond the political boundaries of Herod.[74]

---

74. Boring, *Mark*, 98; Guelich, *Mark 1—8:28*, 142.

Mark and Aretalogy concerning the Best Folk Healer—Jesus

PRAISE-GIVING CONCERNING THE HEALING OF A MAN WITH A DEMON (MARK 5:1–20)

In chapter 1, we have seen similar healing of a demon-possessed man in the synagogue. What was the condition and how does the story presents Jesus as the healer and what possible aretalogy accompanied the story? Three positions have been proposed regarding the genre of the narrative. First, because of its lack of typical exorcism themes of confrontation and dismissal of the demon, it has been regarded as a tale or novella. In the current passage, contrary to previous exorcisms, the demon talks and bargains with Jesus. Furthermore, given that the demons negotiated to be transferred into the pigs, no clear exorcism is noticeable within the story. The second possibility is that the story began as an exorcism story that was later adopted as a missionary story to which midrash material and allusions to the exodus were added.[75] The third and most recent approach to the story is seeing it as a satire against the Roman Empire. Concerning this, the story, using demonology language, tells about the defeat of the empire from the region which is implied by reference to derogatory terms such as pigs and legion.[76]

I take a medical-anthropological approach that reads the story as an emic cultural interpretation of sickness by an itinerant healer—Jesus. As noted, two positions existed regarding demon possession. The first, associated with the Hippocratic teaching, interprets demon possession as a neurology or some form of disturbance in the normal functioning of the brain. In this regard, the Methodists prescribed various practical ways to rehabilitate the mentally unstable patient through music and accompanying the person to watch entertainment games. In doing so, the idea was to make the mentally sick person recover his normal consciousness. However, the second and seemingly dominant view was to interpret demonology as an evil spirit that evades the person's normal mental capacity, thus making him do things that are weird such as stealing, prostitution, and abnormal conditions such as talking alone, walking or staying at the grave sites. Taking a medical anthropological approach, the controlling and destructive nature of the demon is well recorded in the story. Verses 3–5 give graphic description regarding the condition of the man: "He lived among the tombs. And no one could bind him anymore, not even with a chain, for he had often been bound with shackles and chains, but he wrenched the

---

75. Stein, *Mark*, 247.
76. Myers, *Binding the Strong Man*.

chains apart, and he broke the shackles in pieces. No one had the strength to subdue him. Night and day among the tombs and on the mountains he was always crying out and cutting himself with stones."

The celebration in the story is in the call to join the household in evangelism. Instead of silence, the healed man is called upon to go and proclaim as Jesus instructed, saying, "'Go home to your friends and tell them how much the Lord has done for you, and how he has had mercy on you.' And he went away and began to proclaim in the Decapolis how much Jesus had done for him, and everyone marveled" (vv. 19–20). Boring comments, "The large and influential Hellenistic city of Decapolis . . . became the foundation story for the church in the area."[77] Perhaps Robert Guelich's remark are more poignant: "This story also introduces Jesus' ministry in the Decapolis (5:20) most likely connoting a gentile territory."[78] Following Guelich's remark, the story is an early Christian celebration of the expansion of Christianity in the Near East region. In this regard, Jesus' command to "go home to your friends and tell them how much the Lord has done for you, and how he has had mercy on you" is both a missionary call and a celebratory remark about Jesus' mercy and power.

In connection with this and in agreement with Hector Avalos, a strong assumption can be made that early Christianity spread primarily as a healing movement. People flocked to Christianity because of its supernatural powers associated with healing.[79] Concerning this, the restoration of the demon-possessed man in a foreign land is aretalogy concerning the healing power of Christianity and, equally, the command to go and tell friends and relatives is both an evangelistic statement and praise-giving toward the Christian god. We can imagine that those who praised Christianity for its healing power sung or chanted regarding its merciful god. Similar to Apollo and Asclepius, a merciful god draws more followers and receives more sacrifice. Arguably, the chant "He is merciful! He is merciful! He is merciful!" was an evangelistic chant and praise-giving call. Such a conclusion should be understood from the perspective that worshipping a deity was a performative act associated with music, chanting, and dance. To recapture such atmosphere we should bracket our modern-day form of worship whereby adherents quietly sit and listen to a preacher during Sunday service.

---

77. Boring, *Mark*, 150.
78. Guelich, *Mark 1—8:28*, 274.
79. Avalos, *Health Care*.

PRAISE-GIVING OVER THE RESURRECTED DAUGHTER AND THE HEMORRHAGING WOMAN (MARK 5:21–42)

The healing of the hemorrhaging woman and the raising from the dead of Jairus's daughter are among the pick of showing Jesus' greatness as a healer. In the public eye, both stories supposes a complicated and irreversible condition that would eventually result in death. Stories of resurrecting people from the dead were commonly associated with great gods such as Apollo and Asclepius.

Here, the "resurrection" of the dead synagogue leader's daughter is abruptly suspended by the horrific story of the bleeding woman. In Mark's narrative, the story took place after Jesus had returned from his excursion to Geneserret where he healed the demoniac. Upon return to Capernaum, Jesus was followed by a large crowd when he was suddenly interrupted by the synagogue leader who fell before him and reported about his bedridden daughter (5:23). What seems like a good response by Jesus was hijacked by a hemorrhaging woman who, from the crowd, touched Jesus' garment, making him stop and heal her. Such telling of two stories blended into one story is called "intercalation, insertion, interpolation, dovetailing, sandwiching, interweaving, interlocking, framing of one story by the other" for the purpose of making the stories illuminate each other "often with irony."[80] The two stories have similar motifs of sickness, healing, and resurrection. Inspired by the stabilized field of medical anthropology, especially the view of Hector Avalos, my reading of the two stories focuses on the aspect of healing as restoration of social function and wholeness.[81] However, recently and inspired by ideas from disability studies, scholars such as Candida Moss interpreted the story of the hemorrhaging woman by focusing on both the body of the woman and that of Jesus as porous subjects. Moss claims that, in the story and similar to that of the woman with the flow of blood, Jesus' body is physiologically weak, "he is unable to regulate or control his own emissions."[82] I have a different conclusion from Moss, who thinks that by oozing power, Jesus became physiologically weak, similar to the hemorrhaging woman. Instead, taking a cue from divine healers, especially those who use divination, they heal using a superior form of power. That Jesus replenishes his divine power through prayer is a recurrent theme in Mark's

---

80. Boring, *Mark*, 157.
81. Avalos, *Health Care*, 25.
82. Moss, "Man with the Flow of Power," 516.

gospel. However, I agree with Moss in saying that, in this story, "the body of Jesus serves as an alternative health-care system—free and accessible to the expensive and ineffective physicians the woman has already visited."[83] Therefore, we continue our investigation of the healing stories of the two sick women as celebration of restoration of their gender roles.

In antiquity, to be sick was a doorstep toward death, and healing was restoration of life from death. Equally, the two stories deal with the issue concerning women. The one was sick and could not have children, while the other was young, but the condition of sickness had cut off her ability to be a mother. Like in the previous stories, what was the nature of the disease, how was Jesus presented as the healer, and what is the aretalogy that comes from the stories?

In antiquity, women suffer from several conditions such as hemorrhage or bacterial infection during and after menstruation. A recent discussion from the perspective of medical anthology is the discussion by Elaine Wainwright.[84] Several strategies from popular, folk, and Hippocratic healing methods were used. Concerning popular healing methods, several herbs were used. For example "squill and agnus castus, fumigate and clean the womb."[85] Cucumber liquid was useful to "expel an unwanted conception, an afterbirth or a suppressed menstrual period."[86] In the Hippocratic teaching, Soranus, from whom we know much about women's health, regarded the female body as physiologically different from that of man.[87] The womb was the main factor that made the female body what it is—a deformed copy of a male body. Several myths and explanations were given—for example that the female body is a product of weak sperm or a product of the male's left testicle. The menstrual blood is a clear testimony concerning the complexity and fragility of the female body. The monthly flowing blood is dangerous and if it goes to the heart or neck, it may lead to her death. Within the Hippocratic teaching, especially from the writings of Soranus of Ephesus, the female body should be treated as strange and different from that of man and special attention is needed to its unpredictable variations.[88] Concerning this, Soranus makes important remarks, saying that the female body is

83. Moss, "Man with the Flow of Power," 519.
84. Wainwright, *Women Healing / Healing Women*, 117.
85. Nutton, *Ancient Medicine*, 99.
86. Nutton, *Ancient Medicine*, 99.
87. Temkin and Eastman, *Soranus' Gynecology*, 129.
88. See King, *Hippocrates' Woman*.

sick because "its whole nature will also be subject to its own diseases."[89] The uterus and its associated conditions of "pregnancy, parturition, lactation" makes the female body vulnerable to several diseases.

From Soranus, the uterus can be inflamed from either retaining menstruation blood or shedding more blood than expected. Concerning retaining blood, this could be due to menopause, young age, or due to engaging in physically exhausting activities such as gymnastics. To such, Soranus prescribes that "warm oil mixed with water or from a decoction of fenugreek, linseed, or mallow cultivated or even wild" should be prepared. As treatment, "the labia having been separated, one should pour in the same oil together with an egg, alone or with one of the decoctions mentioned, beaten up to the thickness of glue."[90] Venesection can be applied by cutting incisions on the ankle to ease the pain. A similar procedure was given for inflammation and bleeding from the uterus whereby olive oil was to be injected into the womb.

Concerning excessive bleeding, Soranus believed that it is caused by "difficult labor, or miscarriage, or erosion by ulceration, or a porous condition, or the bursting of blood vessels . . . and the patients become weak, shrunken, thin, pale, and if the condition persists, suffer from anorexia."[91] Such condition was believed to be complicated to treat. As part of treatment, the patient was supposed to lie on her back with her feet raised to her knees. She should be still, lest the blood comes out. In addition, "Clean, soft, flat sea sponges soaked in cold water, or vinegar diluted with water, or vinegar alone should be applied to the genitals, the pubes, the hips and the loins, and later on to the chest too, and should frequently be renewed."[92] In addition, she should be allowed to rest more and have her heals rubbed with olive oil while her face is rubbed by a cloth soaked in cold water. Concerning bathing, she should take "baths of cold water up to the groin, or of diluted vinegar, or pure vinegar, or a decoction of myrtle berries, or dried roses, or 'omphakitis oak gall,' or myrtle and lentils, or mastich, or pomegranate peel, or bramble blossoms, or leaves of oak or of willow, or tanning sumach."[93] If the hemorrhaging persists, the juice of "plantain or knotgrass or endive or black nightshade or fleawort or perdikion . . . the juice of

89. Temkin and Eastman, *Soranus' Gynecology*, 129.
90. Temkin and Eastman, *Soranus' Gynecology*, 137.
91. Temkin and Eastman, *Soranus' Gynecology*, 161.
92. Temkin and Eastman, *Soranus' Gynecology*, 162.
93. Temkin and Eastman, *Soranus' Gynecology*, 162.

hypocist and acacia, as well as opiurn (mixed with vinegar either all together or singly), or omphakion, to the amount of two cyaths" should be injected into the uterus.[94] Due to the condition, so much is blood lost, bloodletting for hemorrhaging patients was forbidden.

The two stories in Mark's gospel speak about women's central role in reproduction. The worst "disability" a woman could have was barrenness. The two interpolated stories in Mark describe women's sicknesses with a common theme of hopelessness to restoration. Within an honor and shame culture, both women had lost their honor by not being able to fulfill their household duties. In addition, due to sickness, their ability to provide children was diminished. At a household level, domestic chores and reproduction issues were the core expectations over women. Inability to provide would result in the husband to take a surrogate wife and having dowry returned.[95] To a woman, losing one's honor within the domestic space would result in one treated as an outsider. In many cases, a continuously sick wife would be taken back to her father's household. While in the case of the synagogue ruler, the daughter was still in the care of her father, it is different with the hemorrhaging woman. Lack of mention of her husband and children meant that her marriage was over and thus, "the woman cannot fulfil her function as woman to bring new life into being as a mother . . . her life is actually a living death and her healing would be restoration to life."[96]

Given that the story clearly mentions that the woman had been to other healers who, in this case, may included the Hippocratic healers, the story celebrates Jesus as a better healer than them. The praise-giving was heightened by the nature of both the disease and the class or status of people that come for healing. The synagogue ruler was a respectable community leader responsible for the daily and financial matters of the synagogue, and his coming to Jesus speaks toward the nature and persona of Jesus as the healer. Concerning this, Boring notices that Jairus is recognized by his title as ruler of the synagogue and that his daughter had a separate room.[97] Second, as noted, the conditions that Jesus dealt with in the story were complicated near-death diseases. Emphasis is given concerning the girl that she was asleep to the point of death. In fact the command *talitha koum*, meaning "little girl arise," speaks to the condition of death. Furthermore,

---

94. Temkin and Eastman, *Soranus' Gynecology*, 162.
95. Shelton, *As the Romans Did*.
96. Boring, *Mark*, 160.
97. Boring, *Mark*, 158.

Mark and Aretalogy concerning the Best Folk Healer—Jesus

Jesus' remark that the girl is asleep and not dead could function as euphemism concerning death.[98] Given this, in the story, Jesus is presented as the healer of complicated diseases and healer who resurrected the sick from the dead. The motif of gods resurrecting the dead is a common motif in Greco-Roman stories. In one story Apollo upon noticing the grieving Admetus, king of Thessaly, who had just buried his wife Alcestis, resurrected Alcestis from the dead and presented her alive to her husband.[99]

This calls for praise-giving in two ways. First, celebrations concerning Jesus as the healer were done over his healing of complicated conditions. Plausibly to both women and their families, they celebrated the healing of their loved ones from conditions that were fatal. The continuous bleeding would have resulted, eventually, in death. Such healing would result in people chanting that "Jesus is the healer of all sorts of diseases." The response by Jesus—"Daughter, your faith has made you well; go in peace, and be healed of your disease" (v. 34)—signifies that Jesus has power to heal complicated sicknesses. In comparison to drinking vinegar and olive oil and having various substances stashed into one's womb, such a pronouncement lessens the shame associated with having a hemorrhaging womb. Jesus' address toward her as daughter signifies her change of status from no-name to being included within the household.[100]

Importantly and associated with the above is the obvious praise-giving that Jesus resurrected both women from the death. No record exists that Jesus was known in Rome as the great healer. However, here Mark claims similar fame of resurrecting the dead which was associated with Apollo and Asclepius. As noted, being sick with such a condition would result in death. In the case of Jairus's daughter, culture dictated that a person should be buried the same day. As such, by the time Jesus arrived, funeral arrangement and processions were already in motion.[101] Upon being resurrected, funeral preparations were turned into a celebratory gathering that sang to Jesus as the healer who resurrects the dead. In a context where sickness signifies nearness to death, resurrection would be accompanied by joyous celebrations, dance, and choral music.

In the commissioning of the disciples in Mark 6:13, Mark defines the activities of the itinerant preachers as that of: healing, casting out demons,

---

98. Beavis, *Mark*, 97.
99. Shelton, *As the Romans Did*.
100. Boring, *Mark*, 161.
101. Boring, *Mark*, 161.

and anointing with oil. The early household church continued doing what Jesus was doing and was defined primarily as a healing movement buoyed by the power of Jesus. Similar to Asclepius, whose apparitions were visible during the night to offer supernatural power to the healing shrine, the household church was empowered by the power of Jesus to heal and to perform exorcisms. The anointing of oil was a post-Easter healing practice which included other rituals such as use of wine. Here, we find the only reference in the gospels were oil is associated with healing symbol (see Jas 5:14).[102]

PRAISE-GIVING CONCERNING JESUS' HEALING OF MANY PEOPLE IN GENNESARET (MARK 6:53–56)

Jesus' second visit to Gennesaret came after the miracle of feeding the five thousand and walking on water. Upon arriving in the region, where he had previously performed exorcism, Mark recounts,

> When they had crossed over, they came to land at Gennesaret and moored to the shore. And when they got out of the boat, the people immediately recognized him and ran about the whole region and began to bring the sick people on their beds to wherever they heard he was. And wherever he came, in villages, cities, or countryside, they laid the sick in the marketplaces and implored him that they might touch even the fringe of his garment. And as many as touched it were made well. (Mark 6:53–56)

Robert Guelich suggests that the passage should be understood as summery report that derived from pre-Markan miracle collections. It contains familiar Markan style whereby Jesus heals people from various cities and towns. The reference to people looking to touch his garment is similar to the story concerning the hemorrhaging woman. Peculiar about this story is that Jesus is the passive character to whom people came to seek healing. The aretalogy portrayed is that Jesus is the healer with fame and has power over all sorts of ailments.[103] In addition, the divine power of Jesus is seen through people touching him and, suddenly, healing is transferred to their bodies. Concerning this, Collins remarks, "The Markan summery shows that the evangelists shared, or at least accepted, the popular belief that the

---

102. Boring, *Mark*, 176; Guelich, *Mark 1—8:28*, 322.
103. Guelich, *Mark 1—8:28*, 355.

healing power of Jesus could be transferred by touch."[104] Boring's comment is poignant when he says, the description is intended to portray Jesus' healing power and divinity whose service to humanity is transforming their livelihoods through feeding and by healing them.[105]

PRAISE-GIVING OVER THE HEALING OF THE SYROPHOENICIAN WOMAN'S DAUGHTER (MARK 7:24–30)

The story evokes debate concerning whether it is a miracle story or an apophthegm or pronouncement. On the surface, it lacks the usual characteristics of a healing story of instant healing. Others have regarded the story as apophthegmatic because, in terms of genre, it combines both the pronouncement and the miracle story.[106] If regarded as healing story, it fits more as an exorcism story in which Jesus commanded the demon of sickness to leave the young girl. Furthermore, the story has been regarded as a quest story in which the quester (women) is set up in the story to evoke the sympathy of the audience with the purpose of seeing if her wish is granted. It is plausible to locate the story in Bethsaida; a place closer to Capernaum from which the ethnicity of the woman is an issue. In addition, Bethsaida is the location that Jesus retires whenever he needs rest.[107]

Mark only tells us that the girl was sick from "unclean spirit." Unclean spirit was attributed to any bodily condition, including fever. To the Greco-Romans and the Jews, any disturbance within the body was attributed to internal inversion by an external evil force and cure was through exorcism. However, the Hippocratic teaching believed that fever was due to bodily fluid imbalance that causes the bodily temperature to heat up in case of high concentration or having lower body temperature in case of low imbalance. In the case of high fever, in addition to certain herbs, bloodletting was prescribed. However, bloodletting was discouraged in case of low blood temperature. Instead, olive oil and staying within a warm temperature environment was recommended. In the case of the Syrophoenician's daughter, we are not sure whether she had a low or high fever, but if she had either, then she would have gone through the mentioned ordeals.

104. Collins and Attridge, *Mark*, 338.
105. Beavis, *Mark*, 110; Stein, *Mark*, 333.
106. Guelich, *Mark 1—8:28*, 382.
107. Collins and Attridge, *Mark*, 365.

Jesus, the Best Capernaum Folk-Healer

The presentation of Jesus as the healer in the story is intertwined with the celebration of his fame. At the onset, Mark announces that when people heard that he is in the house, they flocked for healing. Among them is the Syrian woman whose child was sick back home. She too, approached Jesus from the basis of faith and understanding of his reputation. Instead of Jesus responding in the usual style of instant healing as he did with the synagogue ruler or the demoniac, he backtracked and gave a somewhat "ethnic" biased answer which has baffled theologians for years. Jesus responded, "Let the children be fed first, for it is not right to take the children's bread and throw it to the dogs" (v. 27). I concur with Boring's comment that "Mark included the story because the central figure is a Greek and to illustrate an important aspect of the church's Gentile mission . . . the Markan narrative as a whole moves in the realm of the problems face by the church as it moved from a Jewish sectarian renewal movement to a Christian church composed primarily of Gentiles."[108]

That Jesus can heal from a distance makes him better than other health-care systems where people needed to travel to distant shrines for healing.[109] Healing from a distance also saves time. Moreover, Christian health-care system goes beyond ethnicity and gender. Concerning this, the woman's remark displaces ethnic categories by placing the outsiders inside, saying, "Yes, Lord; yet even the dogs under the table eat the children's crumbs" (v. 28). The dog is metaphor of outsiders and in this case, the Greeks. Her call to have the outsiders inside and to have them eat the same food as the insiders is the praxis of Jesus' healing that is extended to all. Jesus is the healer of all and his power is not ethnically confined. Equally, Jesus' pronouncement, "You may go your way; the demon has left your daughter," sums up the commensality of Jesus' healing. In the story, ethnic divisions were healed and diseases associated with being the other were cast away. Through healing, Jesus created a cosmos based on universal healing which rivaled the Olympian gods and the Titans. In the healing cosmos of Jesus, gender, age, and ethnicity are not barriers to the healing power of Jesus.

---

108. Boring, *Mark*, 206.
109. Avalos, *Health Care*, 100.

PRAISE-GIVING OVER THE HEALING OF A DEAF MAN (MARK 7:31–37)

The two stories concerning the healing of the blind and deaf man form an *inclusio* around the second feeding story and the understanding of the disciples. With common themes, in the stories, Jesus is invited by the community to heal a deaf (κωφὸν) and a dumb man (μογιλάλον) whom he took aside and he put fingers in his ears and then applied saliva to his tongue. The healing rituals seem different from the usual command and exorcism of demons. Concerning this, Boring remarks, "Each story shares standard healing stories in the Hellenistic world, making Jesus resemble the typical 'divine man' of the Greco-Roman world."[110]

What was the nature of the condition and the cultural assumptions concerning the condition of blindness? Among the Jews, not being able to hear was regarded as divine punishment which only God can cure. Thus from a theological perspective, the restoration of the man's sight implies the arrival of divine power far beyond other healers. However, we need cultural anthropological insights regarding deafness. The Hippocratic teaching interprets loss of hearing as a condition that was caused by the imbalance of fluids in the brain. In addition, certain food types such as too much salt in food was believed to cause headache and eye problems. This was also true with eating unripe apples or grapes. For Hippocrates, when fluid accumulates in the brain, it affects ear conditions.[111] In many of such conditions of deafness, no remedy was available. People with deafness faced various social stigmas. In addition to being seen as being cursed by the gods, they could not marry or have children and/or were not considered as normal people. In the Synoptic Gospels, deaf people are always situated at the periphery of society where they begged or relied on well-wishers for help. If noticeable at birth, a condition of being deaf could be reversed by the midwife at the day of birth. Soranus explains that, at birth, the midwife should carefully check that "ears, nose, pharynx, urethra, anus are free from obstruction; that the natural functions of every member are neither sluggish nor weak; that the joints bend and stretch; that it has due size and shape and is properly sensitive in every respect."[112] This may also apply to the comparable story in John 9:1–12 concerning the man who was born blind, since his condition may

---

110. Boring, *Mark*.

111. Nutton, *Ancient Medicine*, 32.

112. Temkin and Eastman, *Soranus' Gynecology*, 80.

Jesus, the Best Capernaum Folk-Healer

not have been detected at birth. For Soranus, there are babies that should be kept and those that should be discarded. In this case, a baby who does not respond through crying or showing ability to see or hear was discarded. In the case of our story, it is plausible that the men who were deaf developed the condition when they were already adults.

The praise-giving is derived from the nature of the condition of deafness. Mark captures the mood or celebration, saying, "But the more he charged them, the more zealously they proclaimed it. And they were astonished beyond measure, saying, 'He has done all things well'" (7:36–37). The term zealously or abundantly (περισσότερον) signifies nonstop excitement, meaning that the man went from place to place proclaiming his new condition. This connects with the earlier motif that Jesus' healing were the center of early church evangelism. One could imagine that in villages where the man used to be known as blind and deaf, people were amazed and joined the man in celebration. Equally, the astonishment (ἐξεπλήσσοντο) of the crowd is a disbelief from seeing such great healing happening to them. Within a mood of excitement and celebration, the remark that "he has done all things" (Καλῶς πάντα πεποίηκεν) well could be read as chanting.

PRAISE-GIVING OVER THE HEALING OF BLIND MAN (8:22–26)

In Mark 8:22–26, we have the healing of a blind man that seems to take double instances of healing. The incident took place in a village of Bethsaida—close to Capernaum. Mark reports, "Then taking the blind man by the hand, he led him out of the village. And when he had spat on his eyes, and laid his hands upon him, he asked him if he saw any thing. And he looking up said, I see men; for I perceive them walking as if they were trees. Then he again laid his hands upon his eyes, and desired him to look; and he was restored, so that he saw them all clearly" (Mark 8:23–25).

Theological perspectives always regard blindness as a metaphor of spiritual condition.[113] Instead, we take a medical anthropological lens that interprets blindness as both a stigmatized condition and a queer condition associated with foresight. Like the previous stories, Jesus' power to heal is known in the village, and upon seeing Jesus, the villagers presented to him a man with the disability of blindness. Like deafness, blindness is associated with bodily disability from birth. In this case, it may imply that the man

---

113. Koosed and Schumm, "Out of the Darkness," 77.

became blind while already an adult. As we explained in chapter 4, here we should notice that cultural stigma regarding blindness differed from that of deafness.

At first, the story confronts us with the popular cultural view regarding blindness. The man is blind and the people had searched for healing and could not find remedy. There is no mention of folk sector medicine of divination, neither the mention of Hippocratic medicine. An implicit assumption could be made that the family may have tried the religious leaders who may have suggested that the blindness is due to some form of divine punishment. However, that the people brought the blind person to Jesus means that they may not have known healing methods. Importantly, the proximity of the village of Bethsaida to Capernaum may have transferred the gossip regarding the new healer—Jesus.

I bring a different interpretation to the condition of blindness by connecting blindness to hopelessness. Among the Dondo people, a person with blindness is a queer character. Blindness is associated with foresight and abilities given of a seer. A person with the condition of blindness can detect and identify people with evil intension such as witches or those who are untrustworthy. We can equally assume that, given that the man had lost his physical eyes, he was now able to see spiritually.

The aretalogy behind the story is the celebration of Jesus who symbolically took the man outside the village where the man was spatially and physically an outsider. An initial healing took place whereby Jesus took saliva to his eyes. At first the man testifies that he sees hazy objects. In what seems like the second healing, the man received his full sight and was taken back into the village. This is the first time that Jesus used saliva to heal; meaning that, besides faith, prayer, and fasting, Christian healthcare system used certain magical means. The fact that the story was left out by Matthew and Luke may imply the hesitancy and debate associated with magical rituals similar to that of Asclepius and the magicians. However, for Mark, the aretalogy associated with the story lies in the instant healing that saves time, and geographic distance.

PRAISE-GIVING OVER THE HEALING OF A BOY WITH UNCLEAN SPIRIT

Form criticism regards the story as composed of two original narratives that were later combined. It is possible that the story of the disciples failing to cast out demons (9:14–20) circulated separate from the story of Jesus casting out demons (9:21–27) and the two were later joined together to prove Jesus' superiority in casting demons.[114] Boring thinks that the story forms the conclusion to the first part to Jesus' public ministry, thus forming an inclusion with the first exorcism (Mark 1:21–27). For him, while the story talks about exorcism, its main themes are faith, discipleship, and prayer that the disciples needed in their defense of Jesus. The presence of the scribes signifies the constant opposition against Jesus and that the disciples need discipleship, faith, and prayer.[115] The disease is regarded as a mute condition which makes the boy unable to talk. However, the description of the symptoms characterized by "seizure," "rolling," and "foam" in the mouth (v. 20) is identical to epilepsy.[116] Pejoratively, the disease has been described as "sacred sickness" because it is characterized by the spirit possessing the victim and making him passive. Other symptoms include being "speechless and choking, froth flowing from the mouth, he gnashes his teeth and twists his hands, the eyes roll and intelligence fails."[117]

What was the cultural perception toward the disease? The story gives clues that the Jews and many other ethnic groups regarded the disease as caused by the demonic force. Consequently, magicians or exorcists like Jesus were regarded as experts in dealing with such issues. Other myths suggest that the disease was regarded as hereditary or a curse from the gods or a condition that comes due to a spell.[118] Because of similarity with ecstatic condition, some regarded the attack as a divine visitation from the gods and therefore, the patient was regarded as having supernatural powers to foretell events. On the other hand, the Hippocratic teaching sees the condition as imbalance of bodily fluid. The healing process may include bloodletting and certain herbs to bring the patient to health. However, as the story recounts, such kind of ailments did not have many successful procedures. In many cases, the patient would die either due to neglect or severity of the condition.

Taking Boring's comment, the aretalogy of the story resides in the faith which Jesus requested from both the disciples and the father of the epileptic boy. The issue can be stated in a rhetorical question: does Jesus

---

114. Collins and Attridge, *Mark*, 434.
115. Boring, *Mark*, 272.
116. Collins and Attridge, *Mark*, 434.
117. Collins and Attridge, *Mark*, 434.
118. Collins and Attridge, *Mark*, 434.

heal all diseases. Mark wants the audience to know that Jesus is the healer of all ailments, including epilepsy, and his power supersedes all conditions. The disciples and all people are called to a life of discipleship, faith, and prayer to a God who is omnipotent. Plausibly, the story would be celebrated as a call to faith and a commitment to Jesus' healing power.

CELEBRATION CONCERNING THE HEALING OF THE BLIND MAN—BARTIMAEUS (MARK 10:46-52)

The story is the last healing encounter and considered as an inclusion that concludes the second section of Mark regarding the Passion prediction and the end of the theme concerning the disciple's lack of faith. Importantly, it looks forward to the destination, Jerusalem, and acts as a call to follow Jesus on the way as itinerant charismatic preachers.[119] Geographically the village of Jericho was the last stop before Jerusalem. Known for its deteriorating infrastructure, the village was dangerous with robbers and hijackers of caravans. However, due to its fertile soils and natural beauty, Herod had rebuilt its eastern part, making it his winter holiday destination.[120] It was common to see beggars on the wayside begging for food and other items. On this day, Bartimaeus, having heard about Jesus, shouted, "Son of David have mercy on me" (v. 46). His use of the title "Son of David" has been a point of discussion regarding Bartimaeus's understanding of Jesus as Messiah, since the messiah was believed to come from Bethlehem. However, his use of the title should not be taken from theological perspective, instead as a designation of respect or reverence. The prohibition by the disciples could not stop him from continuously seeking Jesus' attention. Upon being healed, he followed Jesus on the way to Jerusalem. From a redaction perspective, Mark retold the story as a story of faith and discipleship, pointing out that, like Bartimaeus, the disciples would be able to follow Jesus as true evangelist when their eyes are opened.[121] We have already seen the challenge of blindness as a curse from the gods, which was punishable by death from the midwife at birth. In his case, it is plausible to say that Bartimaeus got blind when he was already an adult.

The praise-giving associated with the story is that this is the only healing that took place close to Jerusalem—far away from the Galilee region.

119. Boring, *Mark*, 304.
120. Lane, *Gospel of Mark*, 386.
121. Beavis, *Mark*, 159.

This is the only named person healed who actually becomes a follower. Jesus calls upon Bartimaeus to follow him on the "way." To follow Jesus is to receive spiritual insight. The context of the story speaks to an image of a religion that was growing and attracting people from various classes—the traveler and those at the periphery such as the blind. Several religions such as Mythraism believed in mystical impartation of power and insight. Later in the second century, we see similar belief systems such as Gnosticism and Second Temple Judaism teaching about spiritual insight. Here, it seems, though not truly mythically, Mark is metaphorically proclaiming that Jesus is the giver of insight. In Bartimaeus, we see aretalogy concerning physical eyes and spiritual eyes, necessary identity markers for itinerant early Christian missionaries.

CONCLUSION

Using the Dondo praise-giving and Greco-Roman praise-giving, this chapter took an imaginative reading of the healing stories in Mark's gospel as celebratory narrative intended toward praising Jesus. The chapter builds upon the discursive assumption given in the introduction that during the first century, cross-pollination exists between other belief systems and nascent Christianity. Furthermore, the existence and evidence of shrines of Asclepius in most villages and at thermal miracle springs makes it plausible to interpret the healing stories alongside other religions. This chapter investigates each healing story recorded by Mark and attempts to give a plausible reconstruction concerning celebrations associated with the healings. Arguably, Mark is deliberate in reporting that Jesus healed sicknesses that were deemed complicated during his time. In each narrative or praise-giving, he is evoking celebration in praise of Jesus. Jesus healed conditions such as demon possession that had robbed men out of their household responsibilities and honor. In addition, he healed conditions such as a withered hand and paralysis of limbs that also took away men's honor. Condition of hemorrhage and several sicknesses had taken away women's gender roles and honor. Equally, conditions such as blindness and deafness reduced several people to non-beings with no value within the household. In narrating each of the healing reports, Mark is aware of Asclepius, Apollo, Machaon, Podalirius, and Hygeia, who had struggled to heal similar conditions. Attributes of power, completeness, and effectiveness associated with the manner in which Jesus healed each of the mentioned conditions erupted

Mark and Aretalogy concerning the Best Folk Healer—Jesus

praise-giving from the listeners who see in Jesus their best folk healer in the village. In each instance, while Mark is calling for attention to the new healer, more so, he is revving up praise-giving.

Chapter 6

Healing Praise-Giving within African Pentecostal Churches

INTRODUCTION

This final chapter contextualizes the discussion regarding praise-giving by looking into healing performances within African Pentecostal churches and how these can, equally, be interpreted as healing praise-giving sessions toward the healer/prophet. Ethnographic work conducted in 2019 from Enlightenment Church form the basis of the data and discussion of this chapter. Available online media material and ethnographic views from adherents contributed to the discussions and conclusion of this chapter. The material is codified and arranged into explanatory variables and, where possible, interpreted using a chosen theoretical lens. The Enlightened Christian Church led by Prophet Sheppard Bushiri is one of the largest African Pentecostal churches in Pretoria. Originally born in Malawi, Bushiri is also well-known for his business ventures into mining, oil investments, and hospitality industry. Furthermore, he is known across African for his nonprofit organization which provides food and assists in humanitarian issues across the continent.[1] Questions that guide this chapter are: during the elaborate healing services within African Pentecostal churches, who is the recipient of the praise? How and what are the nature of ailments being healed and how are they healed? What is the nature or performance of aretalogy?

1. Mantagira, "Man behind the Pulpit."

Healing Praise-Giving within African Pentecostal Churches

Each Sunday, several people flock to his church mainly for healing. After reviewing perspectives regarding healing miracles in African Pentecostal churches, this chapter presents a reading of healing performances as aretalogies toward the healer. Such a perspective takes a phenomenological lens which does not dismiss the healing performances as either authentic or wrong. Instead, it focuses on how the healing stories glorify the healer as more than mere human being, instead as one who is regarded as the embodiment of the divine. Such conclusion is sympathetic to the African view concerning divine men or people such as sangomas who are regarded as possessed by divine power.

PERSPECTIVES CONCERNING HEALING WITHIN AFRICAN PENTECOSTAL CHURCHES

African Pentecostal churches have various possible formative causes. Borrowing from their predecessors who focus on spirit-filled life and the evidence of speaking in tongues, they emphasize more the idea of spirit-filled life by looking into the evidence of the fruits of the spirit. Because of this, three notable perspectives within African Pentecostalism are evident. First, there are those who focus on small or large group family model Pentecostalism (family model) who focus on building strong cell groups that function as mechanism for helping each other economically. Within these groups, members see each other as close family member who provide each other with ideas and networks for survival. Upon visiting such models, you are given an attendance register book where you write your name and contact details and fellow members would visit you. Through this, fictive kinship ties are built. In these groups, while spirit-filled life, evident through speaking in tongues, is central, much focus is on generous deeds toward others.

The second model is the "business model" African Pentecostalism, which takes the form of American talk-show hosts and business language to empower their members. Because of their ability to combine business language and Scripture, these are more successful among the growing African middle class. Typically, their sermons are later compiled into book form or other media channels and sold to church member as fundraising. Some of their favorite topics are: "seven way to succeed," "seven ways to be a blessing to others," or "seven ways to have a happy marriage." Noticeably, unlike their predecessors who focus on the end of the world, these embrace the world and equip their congregants to be successful in life. To these, successful Christian life is seen in being organized in life and hard work.

Of interest to this chapter is the "spirit-filled" African Pentecostalism which seemingly cross-pollinates with African worldview of antagonizing demons. To these, because they embrace the African personalistic worldview, life is a tug-of-war between the mortals and the spiritual world. The spiritual world is full of demons that oppose the goodness of life. Therefore, the task of the church is to cast away demons and healing those who are oppressed by sickness from the demons. In terms of worldview, all social events have a corresponding spiritual interpretation and illness is an indicator.

Among African scholars, three main perspectives exist regarding the healing miracles that daily take place within African Pentecostal churches. These are *psychological view, comparative cultural views*, and the *dismissive "charlatan" view*. First, the psychological view starts with the contextual condition of the people who receive healing. African Pentecostalism breeds in various African societies where there is high unemployment, poverty, poor service delivery, and poor health facilities. In most cases, such conditions lack proper government institutions that keep the government officials accountable regarding the use of public funds. In response, governments such Zimbabwe use violence to silence the people from seeking justice. Within such contexts, healing in African Pentecostalism is a constructive postmodern activity that seeks to find alternative meaning and healing.[2] The assumptions of this conclusion are derived from Frantz Fanon's study in Algeria, where he notes that, within a context of violence the people would divert attention from oppression by believing in demon possession.[3] Similarly, Pentecostalism diverts people's attention from blaming the government of the expensive and inaccessible hospital facilities to seeking help from faith healers.

The second dominant perspective, suggested by Abgu Kalu, proposes that African Pentecostalism needs to be investigated from its cross-pollination with African traditional ideas regarding healing.[4] Within African traditions, healers are possessed by ancestral or alien spirits to perform healing. In addition, through spiritual revelation, the healing process includes the healer performing the role of a seer by telling the patient the nature and

---

2. Dube, "Locating Exorcisms and Faith Healing," 99.
3. Frantz, *Wretched of the Earth*.
4. Kalu, "Discursive Interpretation," 71.

condition of the ailment. Rituals such as commanding the demon, touching and even use of healing items such as oil and water are part of the healing process. From such similarities, Kalu argues that African Pentecostalism is a modernization and adaptation of African healing methods within the church.[5] By using similar healing rituals, African Pentecostalism sanitizes the healing practices that speak to people's worldview and spirituality. Notably and similarly, like diviners, African Pentecostal healers employ strategies of being a seer by foreseeing people's ailments. Holy water, oil, and symbolic cloths are also used.

The third perspective which arises from the several sexual and financial abuses allegedly committed within the African Pentecostal churches raise eyebrows and questions concerning the legitimacy and spirituality associated with certain practices within African Pentecostal churches. From studies done in Zambia, Naomi Haynes highlighted the material inequality perpetuated by some African Pentecostals who drive expensive cars and live in luxurious houses at the expense of their congregations. While in her article she focuses on emerging social kinship ties within the churches, equally, she notices the spirituality around the teaching concerning prosperity which makes the pastors rich while the poor are labeled as lacking in faith.[6] Similar observations are noticeable in South Africa where several African preachers such as Shepard Bushiri and Prophet Mboro are millionaires at the expense of their congregations.[7]

I take a different perspective inspired by the views of Hector Avalos that says that African Pentecostal churches present an alternative healthcare system that, from people's eyes, is free of charge, characterized by instant healing, and less rituals. More importantly, similar to visiting a sangoma, African Pentecostalism presents a "divine man" character in the form of a prophet. The praise given to Prophet Bushiri is based on nature or kind of healing performed. As background, seen from various hymnal and choral songs, Christianity always positions itself as a healing religion. Equally, the arrival of Protestant and Pentecostal Christianity heralded a new form of healing based on the name of Jesus of Nazareth. Given that African traditional religion sees other religions as complementary healing or belief practices, the arrival of Jesus the healer was welcomed by all. Having settled among the African people, the people needed to make sense of

5. Kalu, "Discursive Interpretation," 71.
6. Haynes, "Pentecostalism and the Morality of Money," 123.
7. Dube, "Ritual Healing Theory," 479.

the identity of Jesus as healer. Earlier interactions were not smooth, since Jesus was packaged as imperialist and one who had nothing to do with African culture. Consequently, schisms from Protestant churches such as Methodists and Lutherans happened. In addition, frictions that ended up in schisms happened in the Roman Catholic Church. In Southern Africa, African independent churches such as Zion Christian Church, Shembe Church, Masowe, and Mwazha emerged due to schisms. Among their grievances was contextualization of healing practices within the African context. Noticeable in these movements, divination, foretelling, and casting away of evil spells is practiced. However, because they take the form of understanding Jesus as itinerant preacher who does not want the Western form of church building, the African independent churches choose to congregate under trees and in open spaces as their venues for worship. Significant in the choice of venue is that, though some rituals are performed in the hut, ancestral worship is mostly done under the tree. The rise of African middle class and the appeal of Western forms of worship, the perception of worshipping under the tree as backward, made people to see the African independent form of worship as unattractive. However, despite the unattractiveness, reports are plenty that people go to Protestant or classical Pentecostal churches on Sunday, but in search of divination, they visit the sangoma or African independent churches during the night.

I concur with Abgu Kalu's insight that African Pentecostalism is sanitation of both African independent and African traditional forms of worship. To proceed, ideas of healing by sangoma highlighted in chapter 2 should be rehearsed here. Sangomas, or traditional healers, derive their powers from the ancestral spirits or alien spirit and, depending on their source, they have different levels of power and healing. For example, a sangoma operating with a mermaid spirit has stronger power, and among other healers, he is seen as the last resort or referral point. Given the similarities between a sangoma and the African Pentecostal healer in terms of levels of power that correspond to the number of followers and honor, I now turn to look into how Pentecostal healers are praised.

PRAISE-GIVING TO THE BEST HEALER—A CASE STUDY OF SHEPPARD BUSHIRI OF ENLIGHTENED CHRISTIAN CHURCH

Prophet Sheppard Bushiri employs several healing techniques: First, he *casts* out demons. In most of his healing encounters, almost all conditions are seen as caused by the demons. In agreement with John Pilch, the African worldview interprets sickness and health from the perspective of culture and not biomedicine. The spiritual world is inhabited by ancestral spirits that are in daily conflict with bad alien spirits. The word "demon" does not fully capture the African spirituality because alien spirits can play positive roles in the lives of people. However, in cases where their power is not harnesses and channeled, alien spirits create havoc. African Pentecostal churches tap into this worldview and provide a holistic healing that goes beyond biomedicine. John Pilch is correct in remarking that ethno-healing practices function to bring the person to restoration with the cosmos.[8]

Second, associated with the above is his ability to *command*. Slight differences exist from exorcism because in command, he can instruct certain things to happen. For example he can say, "I declare and decree that your body is free from sickness."

The third healing ritual is of *hand waving*. While doing it, Bushiri gestures to the affected limb, for example a leg, and shows signs such as scooping or retrieving something out. In doing so, Bushiri indicates that he is perceiving something that people are not seeing. Such gestures show that he lives in the supernatural world.

Fourth, in many of his healing encounters, Bushiri calls upon the patient to *look at him in the eye*. In doing so, he calls for total concentration or attention from the patient. However, it seems that, by looking at him in the eye, he transmits magical power through the eyes. In African traditional belief system, eyes are a widow into the person's soul. For example, witches are known for avoiding eye contact or doing the opposite by looking intensely at their victim. By using eyes as healing ritual, seemingly, Bushiri transmits power from himself to the patient.

Fifth, Bushiri uses unconventional healing rituals such as asking a sick person to *touch his shoes*. However, this ritual is used in many other situations. I noticed that, sometimes, after foretelling events into the person's life, he might end up asking that the person touch his shoes. Such rituals

---

8. Pilch, *Healing in the New Testament*, 68.

seem to suggest that, through touching his shoes, one magically receives blessings or anointing. Generally, there seems to be a belief among his followers that, touching him, one gets blessings. In many cases, while walking along the aisles, congregants extend their hand in trying to touch him.

Sixth, *anointing oil* is one of the major healing rituals used by Bushiri. Depending on needs and strength, there are several types of anointing oil. Some anointing oils are for sickness, spiritual protection, or for general use. Selling of anointing oil is a booming business in his church. Most of the anointing oils have the sticker of his face and the description of the oil on them. Sold at R150 per 100mL, the *Lion of Judah* anointing oil believed to cover all general needs is the most common product. The other common anointing is *Angel Gabriel* oil. Besides oils, Bushiri sells anointing water and wrist bangles.

Lastly, like Apostle Peter in the Bible, Bushiri uses *his shadow*. In doing this, he lines up people on wheel chairs and instructs them that, when his shadow touches them, they should stand up because the shadow imparts instant healing. This healing ritual reinforces the earlier rituals such as touching and looking at the patient's eyes. It reinforces the belief that Bushiri has supernatural powers. Equally, by seemingly repeating the healing ritual performed by Peter the Apostle, implicitly, Bushiri claims divine power similar to that of Jesus' disciples. We now proceed to categorize the various sicknesses and the nature of praise associated with each healing procedure.

PRAISE-GIVING CONCERNING HEALING LEG PROBLEMS

Data in this section was collected through participant observations conducted on several dates: October 20, November 22, and November 24, 2019, and January 3, 2020. During the last visit, on the third of January, I witnessed the healing of a paralyzed girl. The service was already in motion and in what seem characteristic of most healing performances, the patient cries out in loud voice such that he/she disrupts the singing. This time, the congregants were singing and the prophet was walking restlessly close to the podium and then he walked between the aisle. As he was passing by, people were chanting, "Major 1!" While others, as if to touch him, extend their hands toward him. In a sense, the congregants treat him as a saint oozing with divine power. During the commotion due to his presence among the people, a girl shouted, "Major 1, heal me! Major 1, heal me! Major 1, heal me! I have a broken and paralyzed leg." *Major 1* is his stage name. He walked toward the girl who had x-ray papers and doctor's reports in hand. To confirm the condition, the prophet asked the medical doctor to read and interpret for him the contents of the documents. Written on the forms was the instruction that the girl could not walk due to the swollen leg and as a result, she uses the walking sticks to aid her mobility. The prophet asks the girl to demonstrate how she walks and then prays for her. Suddenly, he instructs her to leave the walking sticks and walk by herself and a miracle happened that she could walk by herself. The prophet shouts, "Look, she can now walk, she is running, give glory to God." While the prophet was announcing her healing, the girl was already running down the aisle chanting, "God of Major 1! Am healed! God of Major 1! Am healed! God of Major 1! Am healed!"

This story can be explained as healing aretalogy and as an aretalogy, it is important to explore the genealogy's power hierarchy embedded in the narrative. "Major 1" presents himself in the genealogy of power, which begins with God and then his mentor, Eubert Angels.[9] Hence, the name *Major 1* implies spiritual ancestry or genealogy in which he is the first son. Implicitly, while God is mentioned, the praise is toward him as an individual that is in line of miracle blessings. Such idea of the world that believes in spiritual genealogy exists both in Greco-Roman aretalogies and among South African healers who identify themselves by means of spiritual ancestry. Concerning Asclepius, we noted how his aretalogies were connected to his father Apollo and to the grandfather Zeus. Similarly, from the opening of the Gospel of Mark, Jesus identified himself by means of tracing his genealogy from God and not the synagogue or the temple. In chapter 2, we also noticed that the authority of an African traditional healer depends on the source of power that determines hierarchy among other healers.

On November 24, 2019, two spectacular healing occurrences happened. Normally, churches services are full and those who come late are accommodated outside where they watch the prophet from the television screen. While the church service was in motion, a man sitting in a wheelchair shouted, "Help me, my brother cannot walk and the doctors want to cut his legs." Such a petition expressed a sense of desperation and faith that the prophet can heal any type of disease. Repeatedly the man shouted on behalf of his brother. To readers of the Jesus healing stories,

9. M'bwana, "Uebert Angel."

such events reenact the healing performances of Jesus himself. Seemingly, disturbed by the continuous call, the prophet responded, "Bring him here." Like the previous healing performance, the prophet advanced toward the man and alongside him was the medical doctor who explained the nature of the disease. Taking the medical reports from the man's hand, the doctor reported that the patient had been diagnosed of hypertension and of diabetes making him unable to walk. The patient confirmed his condition with desperate voice said, "I cannot walk. I cannot do anything, I fall if I try to do anything, heal me, Prophet. I believe that you are man of God and everything is possible." His plea echoes gospel narratives concerning several people who trusted Jesus for healing. As this mini-drama was taking place all eyes were on the prophet to see his next move. Seemingly unfazed by his desperate condition, the prophet looked up to heaven, touched the man's head and commanded him to stand up. Suddenly, the man stood up and began to celebrate, saying, "God of Major 1, you are powerful! God of Major 1, you are powerful!"

A woman who shouted, "God of Major 1, heal my husband, he has kidney problems and is diabetic," disrupted the scene. Suddenly, the camera shifted attention toward where the noise came and a man sitting in a wheelchair with a bandaged leg and drainage tube from his leg became the focus of attention. The woman who had brought the man continued screaming for attention. The choir and the whole congregation began singing softly, "You are the God, you are the God, that healed me." The prophet requested that the bandage be opened so that he can see the wound and asked how the tube from the leg works. The fluid drained from the leg was visibly seen as the camera zoomed in on the leg. The interrogations and the visuals heighten the gravity of the problem which correspond to the level of gratitude or praise.

Visibly depressed by the condition of the man, the prophet knelt beside the man's wheelchair and prayed for God's healing and then stood up and stretched his hand toward the man's leg. His hand could be seen gesturing, scooping something from the man's leg, and in response the man's face expressed pain. After several gestures of scooping, the amount of dirt seen in the pipe increased and the prophet shouted, "Be healed, be healed!" Later he commanded, "Stand up and walk, look at me as you walk, walk toward me, you are not going to fall down!" The man followed the instruction and stood up. The man creamed, "Major 1, my papa, am healed! Major 1, my papa, am healed!" The prophet then instructed, "Do one thing for me, come back here Thursday, you will be fully healed."

As an aretalogy, these two events capture the prophet as one with power to heal all kinds of sickness. A deeper meaning is that he heals conditions that modern hospitals failed to heal. This notion connects to the previous idea concerning hierarchies of power which to the prophet, he is celebrated as being more powerful than modern medicine. The presence of medical reports and the summery reports from professional doctors convey the image that modern medicine is less powerful. The acclamation by those healed is a testimony to the reality of the superior power residing in the prophet. In discussing both Greco-Roman healers and Jesus of Nazareth, the motif of a healer presenting himself as more powerful than others is a recurring theme.

October 22, 2019, witnessed four occasions of leg healing. Noticeably, on this day there was no screaming from the patients for attention. However, almost close to the pulpit, the church ushers drive in four people who were in wheelchairs and all holding their walking sticks. No indication that the scene could have been staged. Instead, on the surface the scene showed that the church cared about people with disability and, as gesture of care, wanted them to sit closer to the pulpit. As the service started and people were singing, the prophet moved toward the disabled people. He summoned the camera operator and the medical doctor to come and explain the condition of each person.

First, the prophet attended to the woman whose bones were broken due to accident. In her hand she held an envelope with the radiography scan that visibly shows the broken bones. The prophet did not react by healing her, instead he moved to the next person—a man with swollen legs. The man narrated that he has been suffering for four years and begs the prophet for healing. Next in line was a woman holding a radiography scan and the medical doctor's report that reveals a ruptured tendon on the right leg due to a road accident. She reported to the prophet that she is due for surgery on next Wednesday. In addition, there was a man who could not walk due to stroke and a woman who had arthritis.

After listening to all reports, the prophet explained how the healing process was going to happen. What happened next looked more spectacular than I thought. The prophet said to the patients that he is a man of God and that, like Peter, he can heal using his shadow. To proceed, he instructed the camera operator to detect where his shadow is so that when he passes in font of the wheel chairs, the patients would respond by standing up and walking. The people began to chant, "Do something! Do something! Do something!" The prophet asked the congregation to lift up their hands and asked them if they believe in miracles. "Do you believe in miracles?" he inquired. People responded in affirmation. "I am going to walk and when my shadow casts over you, move from your chairs and walk." He began walking and instructing, "Move out, look at that, just walk." As the miracle was happening, the congregation was screaming, praising the prophet. "Did I pray, I just used my shadow, my shadow is enough," he retorts. Having witnessed the miracle, the congregation began singing, "By your name the blind shall see, the lame shall walk." As the scene concludes, the prophet told the congregation that the venue is holy and full of blessings. Similar to Moses who received instruction from God regarding the holiness of Mount Sinai, the prophet proceeded to ask the congregation to get on their knees and touch the floor to receive their healing miracle. Suddenly a man with visible bandage on the knee came in front and testified that he had a knee problem that made him unable to walk but after following the instruction by the prophet, he bent and his knee was restored. He testified, saying, "I could not walk or kneel down but now the pain has subsided. The pain is gone."

PRAISE-GIVING CONCERNING THE HEALING OF STOMACH PROBLEMS

On October 4, 2019, the prophet healed a man with a swollen stomach. As the church service proceeded, four men carrying a man on a mattress walked toward the pulpit. Commotion could be seen as they proceeded but there was no resistance from the security official in trying to stop the men from entering and seemingly disrupting the church service. In front of the procession was the man's wife, shouting, "Major 1, heal my husband, he has a swollen stomach, he cannot walk, speak, and eat." The prophet allowed the men to bring the mattress in front, but as they were about to lift the man and put him on the ground, the mattress broke. The prophet shouted, "The angel of God struck the mattress." Now the man with visibly swollen stomach was on the floor and the prophet raised his hand over the man's stomach. As he hovers his hand, the stomach is seen decreasing. In respond the people shouted, "God of Major 1, you have done it again." "Some shout, Hallelujah," the prophet said. As evidence of healing, he proceeded to command the man to stand up and walk.

In this healing two issues are being celebrated—first the prophet's ability to heal complicated conditions, and second, celebration of the presence of angels who broke the mattress. The ability of the prophet to heal complicated issues is a foregone conclusion in the minds of the adherents, but to the visitors such miraculous occurrences are supposed to put focus on the prophet. The miracle of a ballooned stomach that suddenly flattens at the command of the prophet is an indelible sight and one that attracts storytelling. In addition, accompanying this spectacular event is the presence of angels. I confess that I did not see the angels and that the mattress may have tone apart due to many factors. However, framing the event as accompanied by the presence of angels makes the event supernatural.

PRAISE-GIVING CONCERNING THE HEALING OF HAND PROBLEMS

On October 20, 2019, the prophet healed a young man whose hand had fractured. He came to church with an envelope containing the doctor's x-ray indicating the broken bone. His hand was covered in plaster and a bandage around his neck. True to his routine, the prophet was walking amid the aisle when the young men gave the prophet the envelop and explained that he was involved in an accident which left his hand fractured. Mostly the prophet walks through the aisles with a medical doctor who took the envelop and interpreted it to the "man if God." The doctor interpreted that the fracture is expected to heal within three weeks. The young man pleaded for healing by explaining to the prophet that he wants to go back to school. In response the prophet says, "Don't worry, God of Major 1 is alive." The prophet touched the hand and stretched it. He told the young man to remove the plaster and find an object to hold such as cup or stone as proof that the hand is restored. "Daddy, the hand can move, no pain, I am healed," the young boy screamed. As sign that he is fully restored, the young man is seen holding a bottle of water and even shaking the hand.

The aretalogy of this event is from comparing biomedicine to spiritual healing. Against the hospital report that recovery would take place within three weeks, the prophet performed an instant healing. Similar comparisons exist with Jesus' instant healing. In this case, the prophet presents himself as an instant healer compared to the hospitals.

PRAISE-GIVING CONCERNING THE HEALING OF CHEST PROBLEMS

Like many countries in Southern Africa, South Africa has hot summers and mild winters which make inhabitants prone to cold fevers in winter period. In addition, working condition in mines and tobacco farms are conducive for asthmatic and pneumonia conditions. Strong health facilities within the country make it easy to deal with such conditions. However, characteristic of government hospitals, congestions and queues provide challenges to effective treatment. Consequently, some people resort to faith healing for pneumonia treatment.

On October 22, 2019, a man holding a doctor's report came to church looking for healing. As the prophet was walking along the aisles, the man lifted his envelop much higher to catch the attention of the man of God. Upon noticing him, Prophet Bushiri walked toward him and asked him to open the envelope and then the medical doctor to read the contents. The report indicates that the man had been seeking treatment for pneumonia for the past seven months. Information was scant regarding why his pneumonia was not disappearing. Was there an underlying condition behind the pneumonia condition? The prophet touched his forehead and commanded, "Be healed!" The man fell down and quickly gained his balance and then confessed, "I am healed, my chest is now clear! I am healed, my chest is now clear! I am healed, my chest is now clear!"

This story has one major aretalogy which is to demonstrate that, in comparison to hospitals or healers where the man sought treatment, the prophet is an instant healer. We witness similar rhetoric concerning Asclepius who was regarded as an instant healer of all sorts of illnesses. Equally, in many occasions, Jesus was praised for being an instant healer. An implicit praise-giving narrative within this story is praising the prophet for his superior power over all forms of sicknesses.

PRAISE-GIVING CONCERNING THE HEALING OF INTERNAL BODY ORGANS

Usually, internal organs are not the common target for miracle healing among most African Pentecostal churches. Perhaps one of the reasons could be that the organs cannot be seen and that it is difficult to demonstrate the veracity of the miracle. However this does not deter Prophet Bushiri from expressing God's power by healing them. Importantly, healing such delicate organs, in my view, is one of the highest expressions of power. In the medical world, internal organs such as lungs and livers could be affected due to several reasons and when that happens, it is mostly fatal.

On October 20, 2019, a man on a stretcher was carried into the church. As the church started, a woman is heard crying, "Prophet, heal my brother, he cannot walk and eat and his stomach is swollen." The man's swollen and protruding stomach could be seen and the man visibly showed signs of difficult in breath. The scene was uncomfortable to look at. Upon hearing the screaming from the woman, the prophet walked toward the woman and said, "Don't worry," and then he walked away seemingly unmoved by the sight. When she notices that the prophet is moving away, the woman screamed higher, "Major 1, please help me! Major 1, please help me!" With a grinning face, the prophet says, "I told you not to worry, but since you continue crying let me attend to you." One of the church ushers is heard screaming, "Major 1!" and the congregants start chanting, "Do something! Do something! Do something!"

With the assistance of the ushers, the man was brought forward and as per custom, a man who claimed to be a medical doctor was instructed to read the contents of the envelop. The medical doctor announced, "Prophet, the man has a doctor's report which indicates that he has enlargements of lymph nodes in the liver due to liver cancer." The congregants expressed shock and empathy. Equally, the prophet is equally seen visibly moved by the man's health condition and instructed the music to stop playing. He knelt besides the patient's bed and began praying for a minute and concluded by thanking God, saying, "Thank you God for healing him." He proceeded by taking the man's two hands and put them on his chest and took a moment of silent and then started blowing air toward the man's large and swollen stomach. From each blow of air, the stomach is seen shrinking and getting normal. He shouted, "Look at that! Look at that! Look at that! Give God glory!" The congregants start to scream in amazement and disbelief.

This healing event praises the prophet as healer of internal bodily complications such as liver cancer. Given that if untreated, liver complications lead to death, the healing celebrates the healer's ability to restore a person back to life. Similarly, in both chapters 3 and 5 we noticed Asclepius's ability to restore people back to life by healing them. Equally, aretalogies exist of Apollo restoring and resurrecting people back to life. In addition, several stories exist of Jesus restoring people to full health. For example, the healing of Jairus's daughter has similar underlying themes of death and resurrection (Mark 5:35–43). A healer who takes people from the brink of life to full life is, indeed, a powerful healer.

PRAISING THE HEALER OF INCURABLE DISEASES

The healing of incurable diseases by the prophet drew attention of religious enthusiasts and government. Like many countries within Southern African who are grappling with high rates of HIV infection, any news regarding cure of the deadly disease receives maximum attention. In addition, fearing relapse by patients from taking their medical prescriptions, the government of South Africa sees it as an offence for anyone to prescribe untested cure over such kind of conditions. Concerning the subject, the prophet declared ability to heal HIV virus and many other deadly diseases such as cancer. Before the November 2, 2019, announcement was made that the prophet shall heal all sorts of incurable illnesses, permission was granted from the local government to perform free HIV testing to all who are willing. In addition to church members, people from neighboring locations who heard the news came. The crucial day arrived and the people collected their results as they made their way into the church. While the church starts at 9:00, by 5:00 the main hall was full to capacity and some had spent a night at the church waiting for the day to come. Provisional tent venues were also full. Those who had tested positive for HIV were visibly seen with posters on their chest written "HIV virus positive" and many flocked to sit at the front seats where they can quickly get the prophet's help.

Upon arrival, the prophet announces that his God can heal form of sicknesses and that, after receiving prayer and deliverance, people who had tested positive should go back and test again because they shall come back with a different results. The medical personnel were given the opportunity to explain HIV virus and that all tested blood was collected with the consent of the participant. Emphasis regarding procedures in terms of how the blood was collected seems to be directed toward unforeseen criticism that the blood samples might be fake or that the blood was illegally collected without people's consent. The prophet took back the mic and declared that God was about to do miracles and challenged all doubters across the globe to bring their patients with HIV virus for treatment. He taunted, "I challenge the world to bring any person who is sick of any disease and has proven medical diagnosis to come and shall instantly heal them." Attention now shifted to the row of people with posters written "HIV positive." To each, the medical doctor read the result and the day the tests were taken and then the prophet laid hands on the person. From lying of hands on the forehead, some patients fall down while others remained standing. Sometimes the prophets interrogated the patients, saying, "When did you take the test and how long have you been carrying the HIV virus." Some had been HIV positive for ten years while others even longer. To each, the prophet, declared, "In the name of the Lord Jesus, out!" Noticeably, the virus is treated as a demonic entity that needed to be cast out. After receiving deliverance, the prophet instructed that new tests should be taken and those who have been prayed for were seen rushing outside for new tests. Noise and screaming started as those who had been instructed to go for new tests came back, shouting, "I am HIV negative! I am HIV negative! I am HIV negative!" The ushers also helped declare the new results, shouting, "Your God is doing it, daddy, the virus is disappearing." As evidence, screen pictures of tests before and after taking the tests were paraded for everyone to see. All those who had been prayed for came back with new results. The celebrations were deafening as some were in a frenzy running and praising the prophet.

The aretalogy or praise-giving associated with such extreme healing is very high since it sets the prophet apart from all other healers. No healer in medical and religious settings has ever declared ability to heal HIV virus. Important to this study is not the veracity of the healing performances but the apparent praise-giving that such healing performances evoke. In the chapter regarding Jesus' healing aretalogies in Mark's gospel, we noticed how Jesus' healing was regarded as unique and powerful. Most of Jesus' healing, such as the casting out of the demon (Mark 1:22–27) or healing of the hemorrhaging woman (Mark 5:25–34), were seen as incurable conditions and by healing them, Jesus positioned himself as the healer of incurable diseases. Equally, Asclepius was renowned for healing incurable diseases. For example in Orr/Hymn 38, with the title "The Sons of Asclepius," Aristides, who later celebrated Asclepius's sons, refers to them as healers of incurable diseases of that time.[10] Given this, the analogue of Prophet Bushiri as the healer of incurable diseases helps us to understand the healer's fame in view of his performances toward diseases that the community regards as incurable.

The motif of fame is closely associated with healing of incurable diseases. By alleging that he has power to cure conditions such as HIV, Prophet

---

10. Russell et al., *In Praise of Asclepius*, 31.

Bushiri is a famous healer, which corresponds to his fame and nature of power. A similar motif is traceable among African traditional healers we have seen in chapter 2. African traditional healers are graded depending on their fame. Healers with less fame receive little consultation, while on the other hand, healers with greater fame are known by many. As indicated, fame is related to the nature of diseases that the healer tackles and importantly, it corresponds to the source of power. The equation of nature of diseases, fame, and nature of power comes clearer in Jesus of Capernaum. Because his power was from God, Jesus could heal any condition and had fame throughout Capernaum and surrounding Galilean villages. This makes us realize that aretalogy or praise-giving is celebration of healing based by acknowledging the kind of power demonstrated by the healer.

CONCLUSION

This chapter complements the analogue derived from the Dondo people and that of the Greco-Roman healer in explaining how divine men are celebrated as embodiment of divine power. In the case of Bushiri, he targets conditions associated with the human body. He heals leg, arms, and internal body conditions. In setting himself apart from other healers, he wants his followers to realize that he is the healer of complicated conditions. The gesture of having a professional doctor alongside who reads and authenticates the sicknesses is meant to silence those who may think that he is faking the miracles. However, beyond the question of authenticity, Bushiri wants to be celebrated as the best healer; healer of all conditions. Whether Bushiri's healing miracles are true or not, this chapter traces the important aspect, that is, healers want to be celebrated and set themselves apart from other healers as best practitioners.

Chapter 7

Concluding Remarks

THIS STUDY EXPLORES THE hypothesis that, given famous and vibrant shrines of Asclepius, alongside his sons Machon and Podalirius and his father, Apollo, in Emmaus-Nicopolis, Hammei-Ba'arah, Hammath Gaber, Hammei Livias, Hammath Pella, Hammath Tiberius, Killirhoe, and the waters of Asia, it is plausible to read the healing stories in Mark's gospel alongside praise-giving attributed to such gods. In pursuing this study, this research discovered that many healing shrines existed in Palestine in Tiberius, Gadara, and Bethsaida. These were used by the Jews, Christians, and the people from other religions. This discovery makes us realize that, during the first century and before Christianization of the area, various religions coexisted. People followed a particular religion based on its efficacy of power. Given this, first-century Christianity existed within a context whereby it needed to demonstrate power through healing the sick, promising welfare and protection. This point nudges us to remove our Christian-centric approach when reading Mark's healing stories. As Bruce Malina and John Pilch remind us, reading the New Testament writing requires an emic approach; taking the perspective of the native. Instead of picturing the healing stories as narratives told in solitude, we should imagine them as stories told orally and as public performances.

Thus theoretically, as developed in chapters 2 and 3, the healing stories should be told as celebrations, festivals, and performative praise-giving stories. Again, given our Christian-centric mindset and our upbringing of hearing the healing stories being read by a listening audience in a church, we may miss the mood and atmosphere around which the stories were told and celebrated. By orally, we should imagine the healing stories as memories told by word of month from one person to the other. In small villages such as Capernaum, Bethsaida, and Gadara, the story of a sick person restored to full health would spread across the village within a day. Given context where famous gods such as Asclepius were renowned as healers of several conditions such as demonology, fever, leprosy, and other bodily disabilities, by healing the sick, Jesus attracted attention of many people as Mark claims that his fame spread across all Galilee. In addition, the early Christian movement that had found its base in Capernaum needed to celebrate its own healer.

As elaborated in chapter 4, Capernaum was located at the shores north of the lake of Galilee. It was close to other villages such as Bethsaida and Gadara. Beside the synagogue and being a village, no significant infrastructure was found in the village. Bethsaida and Gadara had thermal hot baths used by the Jews and non-Jews. In addition, the town of Tiberius in the south housed a synagogue and a thermal bath too. Located near the lake, the village was prone to various conditions such as fever. In addition, like most ancient villages, cases of demon possession and disabilities such as paralysis, deafness, and blindness existed. Mark also records women-related conditions such as hemorrhage and other related sicknesses. The scenario whereby people would go to thermal miracle springs such as that at Bethsaida and wait for long hours to receive magical healing signifies the level of desperation for healing. Consequently, the arrival of Jesus as healer raised the fame of Capernaum village.

In chapter 5, we explored Mark's celebration of Jesus as healer. Mark gives clues that through each healing, Jesus' fame spread to villages such as Nazareth, Migdal, Cana, and Chorazin. With analogue from celebration of Greco-Roman heroes and praise-giving among the Dondo people, we have clues regarding how fame was celebrated. Fame was celebrated through choral songs (paeans) and dance. At healing shrines such as that of Asclepius and Dionysus, particular dance performances were done. Taking such analogue of dance, it changes our mindset regarding the form and context associated with the healing stories which, in our modern churches we listen to in a gesture of calm and motionlessness. Contrarily, praise-giving such as that by Mark means that, plausibly, there was public choral music and dance associated with each healing encounter. The context of the village of Capernaum whereby few rich people lived, suits choral dance performances. For example, the healing of the demoniac would be followed by public street performance. Given the context, it is unimaginable that the

Concluding Remarks

relatives who accompanied the once demon-possessed man to the synagogue were silent on their return to the village (Mark 1:23). Equally, the healing of several people that gathered at Peter's mother-in-law after hearing of the healings, cannot be imagined as a silent audience (Mark 1:28). The man who was suddenly healed of leprosy did not quietly find his way to his home (Mark 1:40). Similarly, the paralytic man and the man whose withered hand was restored would not bother themselves with the subsequent debate regarding the Sabbath (Mark 2:1—3:6). Furthermore, while the woman with hemorrhage did not silently find her way to her husband after the healing, Jairus, whose daughter was raised from the dead, did not keep it a secret (Mark 5). The man from whom Jesus casts away demons would not keep such a great recovery a secret. Similar conclusions can be said concerning the Syrophoenician woman, the blind man, and the deaf man, Bartimaeus, the paralytic at Bethsaida, and the blind man at Jericho—all celebrated their recovery with their household members and with the Jesus movement in Capernaum. A performative approach to the healing stories shows that Jesus was celebrated as the healer within the context of other healers and that, to the Jesus movement, his healings had identity formation of celebrating the best folk healer of Capernaum.

Bibliography

Abdelwahed, Youssri. "Two Festivals of the God Serapis in Greek Papyri." *Rosetta* 18 (2016) 1–15.
Achtemeier, Paul J. "Gospel Miracle Tradition and the Divine Man." *Interpretation* 26 (1972) 174–97.
Alexander, Jeffrey C., et al. *Cultural Trauma and Collective Identity*. Berkeley: University of California Press, 2004.
Assmann, Jan, and John Czaplicka. "Collective Memory and Cultural Identity." *New German Critique* 65 (1995) 125–33.
Avalos, Hector. *Health Care and the Rise of Christianity*. Peabody: Hendrickson, 1999.
Baden, Joel S., and Candida R. Moss. "The Origin and Interpretation of Ṣāraʿat in Leviticus 13–14." *Journal of Biblical Literature* 130 (2011) 643–62.
Baergen, Rene Alexander. *Re-placing the Galilean Jesus: Local Geography, Mark, Miracle, and the Quest for Jesus of Capernaum*. Toronto: University of Toronto, 2013.
Bauckham, Richard. *The Gospels for All Christians: Rethinking the Gospel Audiences*. Grand Rapids: Eerdmans, 1998.
Beavis, Mary Ann. *Mark*. Grand Rapids: Baker Academic, 2011.
Bediako, Kwame. *Jesus and the Gospel in Africa: History and Experience*. Maryknoll: Orbis, 2004.
Best, Ernest. *Following Jesus: Discipleship in the Gospel of Mark*. Journal for the Study of the New Testament: Supplement Series 4. Sheffield: Sheffield Academic, 1981.
———. *The Temptation and the Passion: The Markan Soteriology*. Society for New Testament Studies Monograph Series 2. Cambridge: Cambridge University Press, 2005.
Bhengu, Cebelihle. "It's a Miracle, 'Major 1' Can Heal; See for Yourself on YouTube." *TimesLIVE.com* (*Sunday Times*, South Africa), February 8, 2019. https://www.timeslive.co.za/news/south-africa/2019-02-08-watch--its-a-miracle-major-1-can-heal-see-for-yourself-on-youtube/.
Bokser, Baruch M. "Wonder-Working and the Rabbinic Tradition: The Case of Ḥanina Ben Dosa." *Journal for the Study of Judaism in the Persian, Hellenistic, and Roman Period* 16 (1985) 42–92.
Boring, M. Eugene. *Mark: A Commentary*. Louisville: Westminster John Knox, 2006.
Botha, Pieter. *Orality and Literacy in Early Christianity*. Eugene, OR: Wipf & Stock, 2012.
Bultmann, Rudolf. "The New Approach to the Synoptic Problem." *Journal of Religion* 6 (1926) 337–62.

Bibliography

Burnett, Anne Pippin. *The Art of Bacchylides.* Martin Classical Literature 29. Cambridge: Harvard University Press, 1985.

Campbell, David A. *The Golden Lyre: The Themes of the Greek Lyric Poets.* London: Duckworth, 1983.

Clay, Jenny Strauss. *The Politics of Olympus: Form and Meaning in the Major Homeric Hymns.* Princeton: Bloomsbury Academic, 2006.

Collins, Adela Yarbro, and Harold W. Attridge. *Mark: A Commentary.* Minneapolis: Augsburg Fortress, 2007.

Craffert, Pieter F. *The Life of a Galilean Shaman: Jesus of Nazareth in Anthropological-Historical Perspective.* Matrix: The Bible in Mediterranean Context 3. Eugene, OR: Wipf & Stock, 2008.

Crossan, John Dominic. *The Historical Jesus: The Life of a Mediterranean Jewish Peasant.* San Francisco: HarperSanFrancisco, 1991.

Darwin, Charles. *The Origin of Species.* New York: Collier, 1909.

De Luca, Stefano. "Capernaum." *Oxford Encyclopedia of the Bible and Archaeology* 1 (2013) 168–80.

Dewey, Joanna. "Oral Methods of Structuring Narrative in Mark." *Union Seminary Review* 43 (1989) 32–44.

———. "The Survival of Mark's Gospel: A Good Story?" *Journal of Biblical Literature* 123 (2004) 495–507.

Dibelius, Martin. *A Fresh Approach to the New Testament and Early Christian Literature.* Vol. 1. New York: Scribner, 1936.

Dibelius, Martin, and Bertram Lee Woolf. *From Tradition to Gospel.* Cambridge: Clarke, 1971.

Douglas, Mary. *Purity and Danger: An Analysis of Concepts of Pollution and Taboo.* Abington, UK: Routledge, 2003.

Draper, Jonathan A. *Orality, Literacy, and Colonialism in Antiquity.* Leiden: Brill, 2004.

Dube, Zorodzai. "Aretalogy of the Best Healer: Performance and Praise of Mark's Healing Jesus." *HTS Teologiese Studies / Theological Studies* 74 (2018).

———. "Locating Exorcisms and Faith Healing in African Pentecostalism within Constructive Postmodernity." *Pentecostalism, Catholicism, and the Spirit in the World* 8 (2019) 99.

———. "Ritual Healing Theory and Mark's Healing Jesus: Implications for Healing Rituals within African Pentecostal Churches." *Neotestamentica* 53 (2019) 479–89.

———. *Storytelling in Times of Violence: Hearing the Exorcism Stories in Zimbabwe and in Mark's Community.* Riga, Latvia: Scholars, 2013.

———. "Ukutwasa—the Call of a Healer: An Analogical Lens into Jesus of Nazareth in Mark's Gospel." *Pharos Journal of Theology* 100 (2018) 1–7. http//: www.pharosjot.com.

Edelstein, Emma J., and Ludwig Edelstein. *Asclepius: Collection and Interpretation of the Testimonies.* Vol. 1. Baltimore: John Hopkins University Press, 1998.

Elliott, John H. "What Is Social-Scientific Criticism?" 1993. https://www.questia.com/library/120090966/what-is-social-scientific-criticism.

Engelmann, Helmut. *The Delian Aretalogy of Sarapis.* Leiden: Brill, 1975.

Evans, Craig A. *Mark 8:27—16:20.* Vol. 34B. Grand Rapids: Zondervan Academic, 2018.

———. "Mark's Incipit and the Priene Calendar Inscription: From Jewish Gospel to Greco-Roman Gospel." *Journal of Greco-Roman Christianity and Judaism* 1 (2000) 67–81.

Bibliography

Felsenthal, Richard Albert. *The Language of Greek Choral Lyric: Alcman, Stesichorus, Ibycus and Simonides*. Madison: University of Wisconsin Press, 1982.

Ferngren, Gary B. *Medicine and Health Care in Early Christianity*. Baltimore: Johns Hopkins University Press, 2016.

Foley, John Miles. *The Singer of Tales in Performance*. Bloomington: Indiana University Press, 1995.

Folkvord, Sigurd, et al. "Male Infertility in Zimbabwe." *Patient Education and Counseling* 59 (2005) 239–43.

France, Richard T. *The Gospel of Mark: A Commentary on the Greek Text*. New International Greek Testament Commentary 2. Grand Rapids: Eerdmans, 2002.

Frantz, Fanon. *Wretched of the Earth*. New York: Grove, 1995.

Freyne, Sean. "The Galileans in the Light of Josephus' Vita." *New Testament Studies* 26 (1980) 397–413.

———. "Herodian Economics in Galilee." *Modelling Early Christianity: Social-Scientific Studies of the New Testament in Its Context*, edited by Philip F. Esler, 23–46. London: Routledge, 1995.

Furley, William D., and Jan Maarten Bremer. *Greek Hymns*. Heidelberg: Mohr Siebek, 2001.

Gerhardsson, Birger. *Memory and Manuscript: Oral Tradition and Written Transmission in Rabbinic Judaism and Early Christianity*. Translated by E. J. Sharpe. Grand Rapids: Eerdmans, 1998.

Giles, David. *Illusions Immortality: A Psychology of Fame and Celebrity*. Melbourne: Macmillan International Higher Education, 2000.

Goldin, Judah. "On Honi the Circle-Maker: A Demanding Prayer." *Harvard Theological Review* 56 (1963) 233–37.

Gould, Richard A., and Patty Jo Watson. "A Dialogue on the Meaning and Use of Analogy in Ethnoarchaeological Reasoning." *Journal of Anthropological Archaeology* 1 (1982) 355–81.

Guelich, Robert A. *Mark 1—8:28*. Word Biblical Commentary 34A. Waco, TA: Word, 1989.

Hanson, Kenneth C. "The Galilean Fishing Economy and the Jesus Tradition." *BTB* 27 (1997) 99–111.

Hanson, Kenneth C., and Douglas E. Oakman. *Palestine in the Time of Jesus: Social Structures and Social Conflicts*. Minneapolis: Fortress, 1998.

Haynes, Naomi. "Pentecostalism and the Morality of Money: Prosperity, Inequality, and Religious Sociality on the Zambian Copperbelt." *Journal of the Royal Anthropological Institute* 18 (2012) 123–39.

Horsley, Richard A. *Galilee: History, Politics, People*. London: Bloomsbury, 1995.

———. *Hearing the Whole Story: The Politics of Plot in Mark's Gospel*. Louisville: Westminster John Knox, 2001.

Horsley, Richard A., and Neil Asher Silberman. *The Message and the Kingdom: How Jesus and Paul Ignited a Revolution and Transformed the Ancient World*. Minneapolis: Fortress, 2002.

Kalu, Ogbu U. "A Discursive Interpretation of African Pentecostalism." *Fides et Historia* 41 (2009) 71.

Kantzios, Ippokratis. "Victory, Fame and Song in Pindar's Odes." *International Journal of the History of Sport* 21 (2004) 109–17.

Bibliography

Kaschula, Russell H. "Imbongi and Griot: Toward a Comparative Analysis of Oral Poetics in Southern and West Africa." *Journal of African Cultural Studies* 12 (1999) 55–76.

———. "Imbongi in Profile." *English in Africa* 20 (1993) 65–76.

Kaschula, Russell H., and Samba Diop. "Political Processes and the Role of the Imbongi and Griot in Africa." *South African Journal of African Languages* 20 (2000) 13–28.

Kee, Howard Clark. *Community of the New Age: Studies in Mark's Gospel*. Nabpr Dissertation Series 6. Macon, GA: Mercer University Press, 1983.

Kelber, Werner H. *Mark's Story of Jesus*. Minneapolis: Fortress, 1979.

King, Helen. *Hippocrates' Woman: Reading the Female Body in Ancient Greece*. London: Routledge, 2002.

Kloppenborg, John S. *The Tenants in the Vineyard: Ideology, Economics, and Agrarian Conflict in Jewish Palestine*. Wissenschaftliche Untersuchungen zum Neuen Testament 195. Heidelberg: Mohr Siebeck, 2006.

Koenig, John. *Rediscovering New Testament Prayer: Boldness and Blessing in the Name of Jesus*. Eugene, OR: Wipf & Stock, 2004.

Koosed, Jennifer L., and Darla Schumm. "Out of the Darkness: Examining the Rhetoric of Blindness in the Gospel of John." In *Disability in Judaism, Christianity, and Islam*, edited by Darla Schummand Michael J. Stoltzfus, 77–92. New York: Springer, 2011.

Kresse, Kai. "Izibongo—the Political Art of Praising: Poetical Socio-regulative Discourse in Zulu Society." *Journal of African Cultural Studies* 11 (1998) 171–96.

Lane, William L. *The Gospel of Mark*. Grand Rapids: Eerdmans, 1974.

Lattimore, Richmond. *Greek Lyrics*. Chicago: University of Chicago Press, 2013.

Lyman, R. Lee, and Michael J. O'brien. "The Direct Historical Approach, Analogical Reasoning, and Theory in Americanist Archaeology." *Journal of Archaeological Method and Theory* 8 (2001) 303–42.

MacGonagle, Elizabeth. *Crafting Identity in Zimbabwe and Mozambique*. Rochester Studies in African History and the Diaspora 30. New York: University Rochester Press, 2007.

Magesa, Laurenti. *African Religion: The Moral Traditions of Abundant Life*. Maryknoll: Orbis, 2014.

Malbon, Elizabeth Struthers. "The OIKIA AUTOU: Mark 2: 15 in Context." *New Testament Studies* 31 (1985) 283–84.

Malina, Bruce J. *The Social Gospel of Jesus: The Kingdom of God in Mediterranean Perspective*. Minneapolis: Fortress, 2001.

Marshall, P. David. *Celebrity and Power: Fame in Contemporary Culture*. Minneapolis: University of Minnesota Press, 2014.

Marxen, Willi. *Mark, the Evangelist: Studies on the Redacton History of the Gospel*. Nashville: Abingdon, 1969.

Matangira, Lungelo. "The Man behind the Pulpit: Who Is Shepherd Bushiri?" *EWN*, 2019. https://ewn.co.za/2019/02/04/the-man-behind-the-pulpit-key-facts-on-shepherd-bushiri.

Mattila, Sharon Lea. "Inner Village Life in Galilee: A Diverse and Complex Phenomenon." *Galilee in the Late Second Temple and Mishnaic Periods* 1 (2014) 312–45.

M'bwana Lloyd. "Uebert Angel Son Perform Miracles at Prophet Bushiri Church." *Maravi Post* (Malawi), July 13, 2019. https://www.maravipost.com/uebert-angel-son-perform-miracles-at-prophet-bushiri-church/.

McCasland, S. Vernon. "The Asklepios Cult in Palestine." *Journal of Biblical Literature* (1939) 221–27.

Bibliography

McGinley, Laurence J. "Form-Criticism of the Synoptic Healing Narratives." *Theological Studies* 2 (1941) 451–80.
M'bwana, Lloyd. "Uebert Angel Son Perform Miracles at Prophet Bushiri Church." *Maravi Post*, July 13, 2019. https://www.maravipost.com/uebert-angel-son-perform-miracles-at-prophet-bushiri-church/.
Miller, Andrew M. *From Delos to Delphi: A Literary Study of the Homeric Hymn to Apollo*. Leiden: Brill, 1986.
Mitchell, Margaret M. "Patristic Counter-Evidence to the Claim That 'The Gospels Were Written for All Christians.'" *New Testament Studies* 51 (2005) 36–79.
Moreland, Milton. "The Galilean Response to the Earliest Christianity: A Cross-Cultural Study of the Subsistence Ethics." In *Religion and Society in Roman Palestinian: Old and New Approaches*, edited by D. R. Edwards, 37–48. New York: Routledge, 2004.
Moss, Candida R. "The Man with the Flow of Power: Porous Bodies in Mark 5:25–34." *Journal of Biblical Literature* 129 (2010) 507–19.
Moxnes, Halvor. *Putting Jesus in His Place: A Radical Vision of Household and Kingdom*. Louisville: Westminster John Knox, 2003.
Mugambi, Jesse Ndwiga Kanyua. *The African Heritage and Contemporary Christianity*. Nairobi: Longman Kenya, 1989.
Mutambirwa, Jane. "Pregnancy, Childbirth, Mother and Child Care among the Indigenous People of Zimbabwe." *International Journal of Gynecology and Obstetrics* 23 (1985) 275–85.
Myers, Ched. *Binding the Strong Man: A Political Reading of Mark's Story of Jesus*. Maryknoll: Orbis, 2019.
Neyrey, Jerome H., and Bruce J. Malina. *Calling Jesus Names: The Social Value of Labels in Matthew*. San Francisco: Polebridge, 1988.
Nisetich, Frank J. *Pindar's Victory Songs*. Baltimore: Johns Hopkins University Press, 1980.
Nutton, Vivian. *Ancient Medicine*. London: Routledge, 2012.
Nutzman, Megan S. "'In This Holy Place': Incubation at Hot Springs in Roman and Late Antique Palestine." *Gods, Objects, and Ritual Practice* 1 (2017) 281.
Oakman, Douglas E. *Jesus and the Peasants*. Matrix: The Bible in Mediterranean Context 4. Eugene, OR: Wipf & Stock, 2008.
Olupona, Jacob Kehinde. "Some Notes on Animal Symbolism in African Religion and Culture." *Anthropology and Humanism* 18 (1993) 3–12.
Opland, Jeff. "Structural Patterns in the Performance of a Xhosa Izibongo." *Comparative Literature* 48 (1996) 94–127.
———. *Xhosa Poets and Poetry*. Arcadia, South Africa: New Africa, 1998.
Parry, Milman, and Adam Parry. *The Making of Homeric Verse: The Collected Papers of Milman Parry*. Oxford: Oxford University Press, 1987.
Pilch, John J. *Healing in the New Testament: Insights from Medical and Mediterranean Anthropology*. Minneapolis: Fortress, 2000.
Preuss, Julius. *Biblical and Talmudic Medicine*. Lanham, MD: Aronson, 2004.
Quintilian. *The Orator's Education*. Cambridge: Harvard University Press, 2002.
Rajak, Tessa. *Josephus*. London: Bristol Classical, 2002.
Reed, Jonathan L. *Archaeology and the Galilean Jesus: A Re-examination of the Evidence*. London: Black, 2002.
Rhoads, David M. "Performance Criticism: An Emerging Methodology in Second Testament Studies—Part II." *Biblijski Pogledi* 23 (2015) 121–52.

Bibliography

Rhoads, David M., et al. *Mark as Story: An Introduction to the Narrative of a Gospel.* Minneapolis: Fortress, 2012.

Robbins, Emmet. "Public Poetry." In *A Companion to the Greek Lyric Poets*, 221–87. Leiden: Brill, 1997.

Rosner, Fred. *Medicine in the Bible and the Talmud: Selections from Classical Jewish Sources.* Library of Jewish Law and Ethics 5. New York: Ktav, 1995.

Russell, Donald A., et al. *In Praise of Asclepius: Aelius Aristides, Selected Prose Hymns.* Heidelberg: Mohr Siebeck, 2016.

Seleka, Ntwaagae. "Hoax Resurrection: Commission Wants to Resuscitate Case against Pair Linked to Pastor Lukau." *News24.com*, July 25, 2019. https://www.news24.com/news24/southafrica/news/hoax-resurrection-commission-wants-to-resuscitate-case-against-pair-linked-to-pastor-lukau-20190725.

Shelton, Jo-Ann. *As the Romans Did: A Sourcebook in Roman Social History.* Oxford: Oxford University Press, 1998.

Solevåg, Anna Rebecca. *Negotiating the Disabled Body: Representations of Disability in Early Christian Texts.* Early Christianity and Its Literature 23. Atlanta: SBL, 2018.

Sperber, Daniel. "The Centurion as a Tax-Collector." *Latomus* 28 (1969) 186–88.

Stein, Robert H. *Mark.* Grand Rapids: Baker Academic, 2008.

Stewart, Eric. *Gathered around Jesus: An Alternative Spatial Practice in the Gospel of Mark.* Eugene, OR: Cascade, 2009.

Stewart, A. F. "Pindaric 'Dikē' and the Temple of Zeus at Olympia on JSTOR." *Classical Antiquity* 2 (1983) 133–44.

Temkin, Owsei, and Nicholson J. Eastman. *Soranus' Gynecology.* Baltimore: John Hopkins University Press, 1991.

Thatcher, Tom. *Jesus, the Voice, and the Text: Beyond the Oral and Written Gospel.* Waco, TX: Baylor University Press, 2008.

Theissen, Gerd. *The First Followers of Jesus: A Sociological Analysis of the Earliest Christianity.* London: SCM, 1978.

———. *The Gospels in Context.* London: Bloomsbury, 2004.

Thompson, Robin. "Healing at the Pool of Bethesda: A Challenge to Asclepius?" *Bulletin for Biblical Research* 27 (2017) 65–84.

Van Aarde, Andries G. *Fatherless in Galilee: Jesus as Child of God.* London: Bloomsbury, 2001.

Van der Loos, Hendrik. *The Miracles of Jesus.* Supplements to Novum Testamentum 9. Leiden: Brill Archive, 1965.

Van Eck, Ernest. "Galilea En Jerusalem as Narratologiese Ruimtes in Die Markusevangelie: 'n Kontinuering van Die Lohmeyer-Lightfoot-Marxsen Ketting." *HTS Teologiese Studies/Theological Studies* 44 (1988) 139–63.

———. *Galilee and Jerusalem in Mark's Story of Jesus: A Narratological and Social Scientific Reading.* Periodical Section of the Nederduitsch Hervormde Kerk van Afrika, 1995.

Van Horn, Nathan W. "By Whose Authority? Narrative Characterization and the Rhetorical Aims of Mark's Gospel in Its Socio-Historical Setting." MA diss., New Orleans Baptist Theological Seminary, 2010. https://search.proquest.com/docview/863833903/abstract/9DCB4AFF65C84CE5PQ/1.

Vergados, Athanassios. *The "Homeric Hymn to Hermes": Introduction, Text and Commentary.* Berlin: de Gruyter, 2012.

Wainwright, Elaine. *Women Healing / Healing Women: The Genderisation of Healing in Early Christianity.* London: Routledge, 2017.

Bibliography

Winn, Adam. *The Purpose of Mark's Gospel: An Early Christian Response to Roman Imperial Propaganda.* Wissenschaftliche Untersuchungen Zum Neuen Testament 2. Heidelberg: Mohr Siebeck, 2008.

Zangenberg, Jürgen, et al. *Religion, Ethnicity, and Identity in Ancient Galilee: A Region in Transition.* Heidelberg: Mohr Siebeck, 2007.

Zeichmann, Christopher B. "Capernaum: A 'Hub' for the Historical Jesus or the Markan Evangelist?" *Journal for the Study of the Historical Jesus* 15 (2017) 147–65.

www.ingramcontent.com/pod-product-compliance
Lightning Source LLC
Chambersburg PA
CBHW071456150426
43191CB00008B/1366